# Ukrain

## drawn thread **embroidery**

MEREZHKA POLTAVSKA • МЕРЕЖКА ПОЛТАВСЬКА

Yvette Stanton

vetty creations

First published by Vetty Creations 2007
Reprinted 2007, 2008 (twice), 2011

Vetty Creations, PO Box 1723, Hornsby Westfield NSW 1635, Australia
www.vettycreations.com.au



**Cataloguing-in-publication data**
Stanton, Yvette, 1974–
Ukrainian drawn thread embroidery: Merezhka Poltavska

1st ed.
48p.; 28cm.
Includes index.
ISBN 978-0-9757677-1-9

1. Embroidery – Ukraine. 2. Embroidery – Patterns. 3. Drawn work – Handbooks, manuals etc. I. Title.

746.44



ACKNOWLEDGMENTS
Many people have helped with this book, sharing knowledge, and giving advice, assistance and support. To each of you I am very grateful:

John Stanton, Lubow Wolynetz and all at the Ukrainian Museum in New York, Tania Diakiw O'Neill, Laura Leverton, Wheat Carr, Prue Scott, Marion Gattung, Hanka Robertson, Rena Holma, John O'Leary, Jeanine Robertson, Elizabeth Prickett, Margaret Fisher, Cheryl Armstrong, Cathy Barzyk, Fiona Mason.

Thank you also to the people of Poltava in Ukraine who developed such an exquisite form of embroidery that I am privileged to now share with others.

My embroidery is an act of worship to God, the creator of all things.

**Photo Credits**
All photographs © Yvette Stanton 2007.
All photographs on pages 5, 6 and 9 are of items from the folk art collection of the Ukrainian Museum, New York USA (UMNY). Item accession numbers are included at the end of each caption.

OTHER BOOKS BY YVETTE STANTON
*The Left-Handed Embroiderer's Companion: a Step-by-Step Stitch Dictionary*
*The Right-Handed Embroiderer's Companion: a Step-by-Step Stitch Dictionary*
*Elegant Hardanger Embroidery: A Step-by-Step Manual for Beginners to Advanced*
*Mountmellick Embroidery: Inspired by Nature* (with Prue Scott)

FOR JOHN, EMMA AND IONA

# Contents

CHAPTER 1

# Before you begin

# Introduction

Ukraine has a long history of embroidery traditions forming a rich part of their cultural heritage. These traditions include both coloured embroidery and whitework, which are often employed to decorate the traditional folk dress and ceremonial linen such as rushnyky (ritual cloths).

Merezhka (мережка), which is sometimes transliterated as myreshka or myreschka, is a Ukrainian word for drawn thread embroidery, where threads are cut and withdrawn, and the remaining threads are stitched to form patterns.

Different regions of Ukraine have their own styles of merezhka. Merezhka Poltavska (мережка полтавська), or Poltavian merezhka, is a style originating from the city of Poltava in eastern Ukraine. It is a whitework embroidery that uses a unique drawn thread technique.

On historical items of Ukrainian embroidery, merezhka is usually used in conjunction with other forms of embroidery. Poltava also has a style of cutwork that is very similar in appearance to Hardanger embroidery from Norway, as is evident in the example below.

There are a number of variations of how to create Merezhka Poltavska. Two main variations, large scale and small scale merezhka, are explained in this book.

Rushnyky (the plural of rushnyk) are long narrow pieces of fabric, featuring a number of different styles of traditional embroidery in bands across the width of the fabric. A rushnyk from the Poltava region could include merezhka, cross stitch and cutwork. Because they are often worked on larger counts of fabric, rushnyky usually employ the large scale merezhka technique.

Merezhka Poltavska was used on shirts of both regular and full body length. They were made of closely woven, fine linen, to provide warmth and aid modesty. Because of the finely woven fabric, they usually employed the small scale merezhka technique. The merezhka was featured in places such as in bands on the sleeve cuffs, at the top of the sleeves, just above the hems, and on the neckband.

### WOMAN'S SHIRT

Poltava oblast, Eastern Ukraine, 1920s.
Body length shirt of homewoven linen, double weave.

**Sleeves ►**

Merezhka (leaves pattern), cutwork and satin stitch (diamonds, eight pointed stars, tree of life motifs).

**▲ Sleeve detail**

Three bands of merezhka. The top and bottom bands use a slightly different technique to the larger one in the centre, as they have no remaining horizontal threads.

The ends of the bands finish with Roman stitches.

**Fabric tuck ▲**

This tuck in the fabric was probably to accommodate a new wearer of shorter stature. The tuck would have remained unseen under other garments.

**▲ Hem border detail (not shown on main picture)**

Merezhka zig-zagging patterns.

**Fabric**

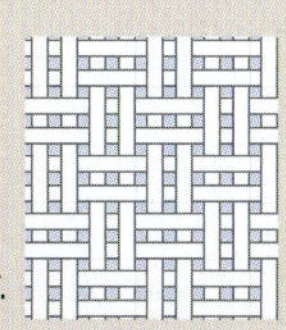

This finely woven fabric has 38 threads per inch. It is a basket weave, with pairs of threads crossing over each other. For thread count, each pair counts as one thread.

89.90 UMNY

## WOMAN'S SHIRT

Poltava oblast, Eastern Ukraine, 1920s. Body length shirt of homewoven linen.

**Neckband ▼**

Tooth edged hem, back stitch, black cross stitch. Shirt sleeves and bodice gathered into neckband. Two sewn loops for fastening with separate tie (not shown).

**▼ Sleeves**

Merezhka band (rose pattern), cutwork and satin stitch (scattered star motifs).

**▲ Sleeve detail**

Merezhka (rose pattern), satin stitch (zig-zags, paired leaves), cutwork.

**◄ Cuff detail**

Tooth edged hem, merezhka (geometric pattern), satin stitch. Sleeve gathered into cuff. Button and sewn loop fastening.

**Fine stitching**

The fabric is approximately 32 threads per inch. The stitching thread is approximately the same thickness, or slightly thicker than the fabric ground threads. It creates firm stitching that is very stable.

**▲ Hem border detail (not shown on main picture)**

Merezhka (smaller rose pattern), satin stitch (zig-zags). 98.52 UMNY

Sometimes the top section of sleeves and/or bodice was made of very fine linen, with the lower part from the chest down in a more economical coarser linen. The fine linen was used for the parts of the garment that were still visible when combined with the rest of the folk dress outfit e.g. sleeveless vest, wrap-around skirt and apron. The coarser linen was used for the parts of the garment that were covered. The hem borders on the coarse linen still featured exquisite stitching even though they only just showed from beneath skirts and aprons.

The fine workmanship of the embroidery aimed to show that the wearer was a woman who was a good seamstress, embroiderer and homemaker and therefore would be an excellent choice for a bride.

Originally, merezhka designs would have been very simple geometric motifs such as zig-zags, and triangles. Swastika shaped motifs were common, as were key (◇◇) motifs. Over time, the motifs became more elaborate, and featured stylised plant forms such as rose flowers and leaves.

## Materials and equipment

### FABRIC

Merezhka Poltavska is worked on evenweave linen. Evenweave linens have the same thread count over both warp and weft threads. Thread count is the number of threads per inch e.g. 25 count or 25 TPI (threads per inch) fabric would have 25 threads in each inch of fabric both across and down the length of the fabric.

To determine if a fabric is evenweave, insert a pin in the fabric. Measure one inch across the fabric. Insert another pin. Measure one inch down the fabric. Insert another pin. Count the threads between the central pin and the other pins. The fabric is evenweave if the thread quantity is the same in each direction. The number of threads in each inch measurement determines the thread count.

#### FABRIC FOR MEREZHKA

These fabrics are suitable for merezhka stitching. Closely woven linens were traditional, but more loosely woven fabrics can also be used. Other evenweave fabrics may also be suitable.

Legacy linen 25ct, closely woven linen. Narrow spaces between thick threads.

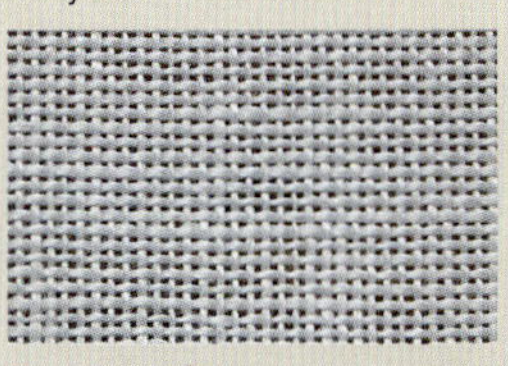

Zweigart linen 25ct, open weave linen. Wide spaces between threads.

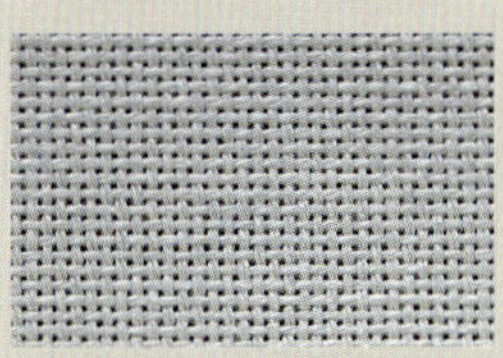

Lugana 25ct, closer weave fabric. Thick threads, with not much space between.

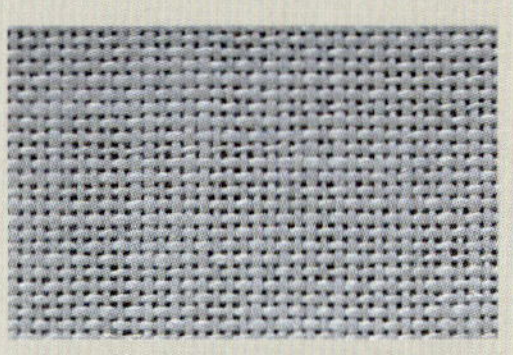

Permin linen 28ct, medium weave linen. Less space between threads.

Glenshee linen (UK) 29ct, closely woven linen. Narrow spaces between threads.

Zweigart linen 32ct, closer weave linen. Tightly woven, narrow threads and spaces.

Some linen fabrics have slubs which are thickenings or unevenness in the fabric's threads. Slubs have no bearing on whether the fabric is evenweave or not.

The fabric would originally have been home-woven. Shirt fabrics were usually closely woven with a high thread count. Rushnyky and other items not for wearing were probably less closely woven with a lower thread count.

Closely woven does not necessarily mean a high thread count e.g. 36, 40, 50 threads per inch. It means that the threads are relatively thick, and the spaces between threads are relatively small. The fabric is quite dense, not gauzy, and not easy to see through. Some fabrics are more closely woven in some of their counts than others. For example, depending on the brand, some 25 count fabrics are much more loosely woven than others. However, in the same brand, a 28 count count linen may be much more closely woven.

The fabric colour was usually unbleached or white, though pale grey, beige, or grey beige were also used.

In order to minimise fraying, it is advisable to overlock or zig-zag the edges of the fabric before stitching.

### THREAD

The thread used for merezhka was a fine cotton or linen single twist thread. It was a non-divisible single strand that does not separate like stranded floss.

It is difficult to specify a thread that is available in all markets, because products vary so much from continent to continent. The following threads are recommended, but may be hard to find: coton à broder (DMC or Anchor), Finca Super (Presencia). Pearl cotton is not authentic but sometimes is all that is available.

#### COMPATIBILITY

| | Thin | Medium | Thick |
|---|---|---|---|
| Anchor coton à broder | 20 (30m/33yd) | 16 (30m/33yd) | – |
| DMC coton à broder | 20 (32m/35yd) | 16 (23m/25yd) | – |
| Pearl cotton | – | No 12 (10g) | No 8 (10g) |
| Presencia finca super | 2/c (757m/828yd) | 3/c (505m/552yd) | 4/c (378m/413yd) |
| Suitable for fabric count | 32ct (approx) | 28/29ct (approx) | 25/26ct (approx) |
| Tapestry needle | No 24 | No 24 | No 22 |

Size/length of skein/ball is included in brackets.

The projects specify threads that are 'Thin', 'Medium', or 'Thick', with the required length. Refer to the 'Compatibility' table above to work out the quantity of skeins or balls needed. For example, 25m of thick thread equates to 1 skein of Anchor coton à broder 12, 2 skeins of DMC coton à broder 12, or 1 ball of Presencia Finca Super 4/c.

Use a thread that is slightly thicker than the fabric's threads to provide good coverage. If your tension is tight, you may need to use a thicker thread than other stitchers – test to make sure. One thread size can be used throughout the embroidery, for both the drawn thread work and any other decorative stitching. Merezhka Poltavska uses up thread very quickly, so it is advisable to use long lengths. However, if you find that the thread becomes furry and fuzzy before you finish it, it is too long, and you should use a shorter length.

To manage coton à broder, remove the wrappers and find the knot in the skein. Hold the knot and carefully shake the skein out so that it opens out into a large loop. Cut the loop at the knot for suitably long lengths of thread.

For the satin stitch or cross stitch designs that are often used in conjunction with merezhka designs, white, black, red or pale colours are suitable.

### NEEDLES

As merezhka is a counted thread embroidery, tapestry needles are used. Tapestry needles have a blunt point, allowing them to pass cleanly between the fabric threads, rather than splitting them.

Choose a needle size to suit your thread. As a guide, the thread doubled over (as it would come out from the needle eye) should be approximately equal to the thickness of the needle. The needle will then create a space large enough for the thread to easily pass through. If the stitching does not sit well or the fabric distorts, adjust the needle size up or down to see if the results improve.

### HOOP OR FRAME

Care needs to be taken with tension when stitching merezhka. The choice to use a hoop, frame or neither is yours. However, if you like to use a hoop or frame for other counted stitching such as cross stitch or Hardanger, you may find it preferable to use one.

If you choose to use a hoop, remove the work from it at the end of each stitching session. Roll the work in a clean teatowel or similar. This will stop stubborn creases from forming and help to keep the work clean.

### OTHER REQUIREMENTS

Most of the projects require a general sewing kit including pins, tape measure, dressmaker's pencil, dressmaking scissors and fine-pointed embroidery scissors. When tacking, pale coloured machine-sewing thread should be used as it will not leave marks when removed, as dark or bright thread would. For construction, hand stitching, a serger/overlocker or regular sewing machine may be used.

## Preparation for stitching

### READING A CHART

There is no standard, universally accepted notation for merezhka charts, so other publications may present information in different ways. If using a pattern from another source, make sure you understand the notation that is used.

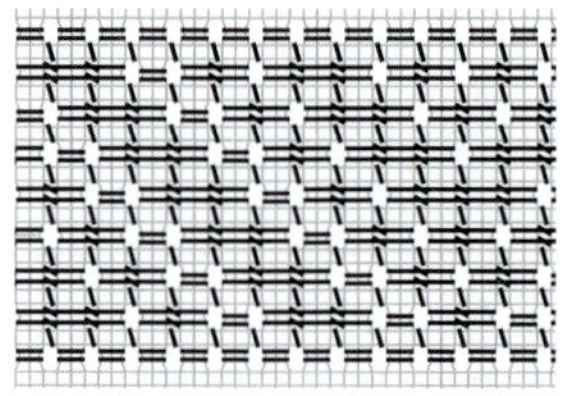

In this book, charts are read as follows. The chart on the left corresponds with the stitched work on the right. The pattern is shown on a grid of squares, where each grid line represents one fabric thread. Each stitch, shown as a thick black line, and its position is clearly shown on the chart, whether it is satin stitch, a Roman stitch layering, a whip stitch or a prutyk hemstitch.

### LEFT-HANDED STITCHERS

Left-handed stitchers can use the instructions in this book with minor or no modification. The stitch instructions will need to either be flipped, or rotated 90 degrees. Any charts or construction steps, such as how to sew a cushion together, can remain as they are.

#### Flipping the diagrams and instructions

The easiest way to do this is to substitute 'right' wherever 'left' is mentioned and vice versa. It may also help to reverse the diagrams. This can be done by holding the page up to a light source and looking at the diagram from the back of the page. You can also use a mirror to reverse the diagrams.

Alternatively you could photocopy the page onto photocopier transparency acetate and flip it over to see the photographs and diagrams in reverse.

## Using this book

Learning Sampler 1 should be completed first, then Learning Sampler 2, to master the two main techniques, before attempting any of the projects. Read through all the instructions before commencing a sampler or project, so you can see and understand the overall process. It is advisable to also practice the additional techniques such as corner treatments on fabric scraps before using them in a project.

If you have any comments or questions about this book, you are welcome to contact me using the details found in the front of the book.

## EXAMPLES OF HISTORICAL MEREZHKA

▲ Woman's body length shirt with merezhka bands on the sleeves (above right) and at the hem (left)

Cross stitched flowers in red and black. Linen does not absorb black dye well, so black often appears as shades of grey. 01.106 UMNY

▲ Merezhka band at the hem of a woman's shirt

This example is unusual because it has double wraps around each of the horizontal bars. The pattern is made of joined key motifs ( ). 93.47 UMNY

▲ Merezhka band with black zig-zag border, at the hem of a woman's shirt

As with many small scale merezhka borders, this band has no prutyk along the top and bottom edges. It has single wrap prutyk for the top and bottom rows, with double wrap prutyk in all other rows. Key and eight-pointed star motifs. 97.66 UMNY

▲ Merezhka band and cross stitching on rushnyk (ritual cloth)

This cloth has large scale merezhka, with double prutyk posts and layerings of three Roman stitches. The ends are worked in Roman stitch. Scrolling grapevine pattern. 97.65 UMNY

▲ Merezhka band on rushnyk (ritual cloth)

Large scale merezhka. The layerings are deliberately worked so that the couching stitches lie in opposite directions for each of the paired Roman stitches (see inset). 78.108 UMNY

CHAPTER 2

# Learning sampler 1

## Large scale merezhka

**This elegant sampler introduces the large scale merezhka technique of Merezhka Poltavska. It is typical of the style used on rushnyky (ritual cloths).**

SIZE 7 x 12.5 cm (2¾ x 5 in)
MATERIALS REQUIRED

- 25 x 30 cm (10 x 12 in) 25 count linen, white
- 23 m (25 yd) Medium thread, white (see 'Compatibility', p7)
- No 24 tapestry needle

## Counted tacking centre guides

**Counted tacking guides are made by counting the threads with a running stitch along the centre axes of the fabric. They assist with the positioning of the embroidery, and can also be inserted anywhere else that may be beneficial.**

1 Fold the fabric in half both ways. Where the fold lines cross each other is the centre of the fabric.

2 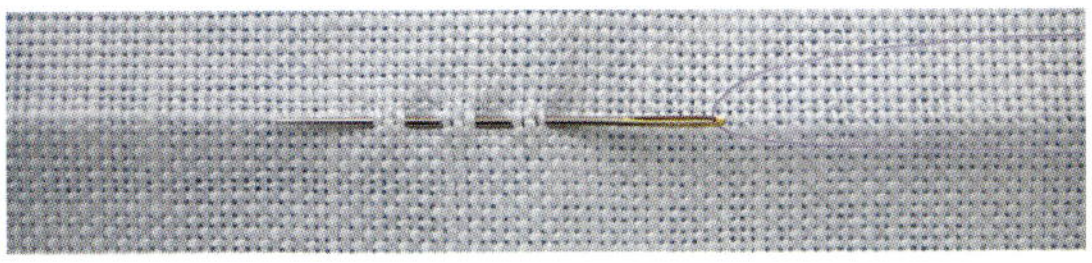

Thread a needle with a length of pale-coloured machine-sewing thread. Insert the needle at the fabric's centre. Working across the wider dimension of fabric and leaving a long tail of thread hanging in the centre, baste under and over groups of three threads. Work out to the edge of the fabric, and fasten the thread.

3 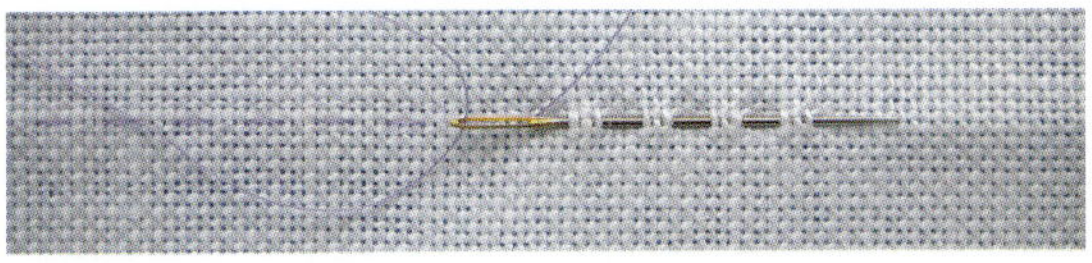

Thread the tail at the centre, and take the needle over and under groups of three threads, in the opposite direction. Fasten the end at the fabric edge.

4 

Insert a new length of machine-sewing thread at the fabric's centre, leaving a long tail hanging. Working towards the top, take the needle under one thread. Baste under and over groups of two threads, fastening the thread at the edge.

5 Thread the tail, and working towards the opposite edge, take the needle under one thread. Baste over and under two threads to the lower edge. Fasten the thread.

6 From the centre of the fabric, use the counted tacking to count 20 groups of three (60 threads) out along the centre guide to the right. Mark with a pin. Count 20 threads up from the pin. Mark this point with a pin. Remove the first pin.

## Satin stitch side bars

**Satin stitch bars form the sides of the merezhka band, edging the threads which are to be cut, so that they will not fray.**

1 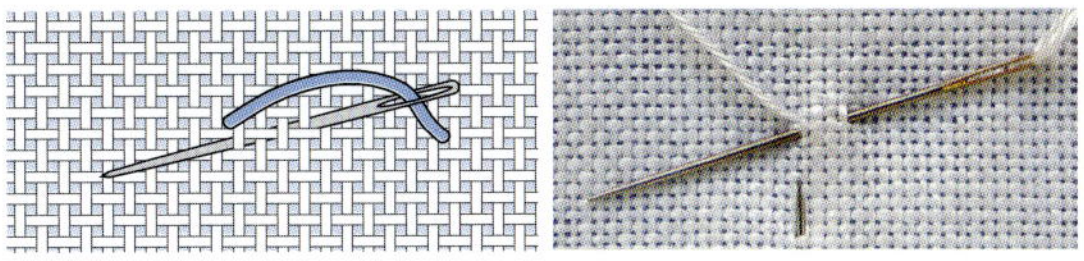

Thread a length of Medium thread. Bring the needle out at the pin. Insert the needle four threads to the right, and bring it out one thread lower than the previous stitch. As you work, catch the beginning of the thread into the back of the stitching.

2 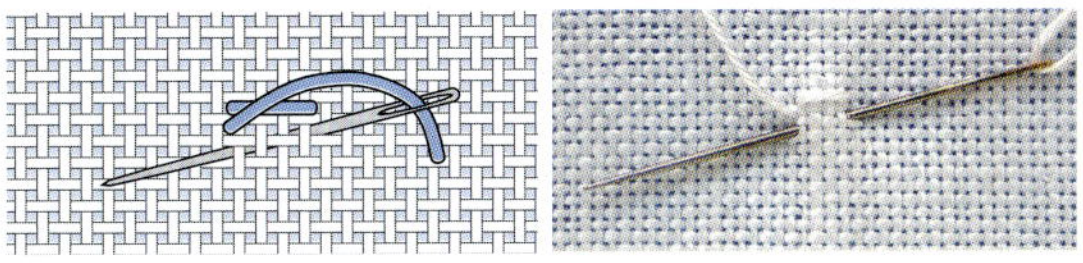

Insert the needle four threads to the right, and bring it out one thread lower than from where it emerged.

3 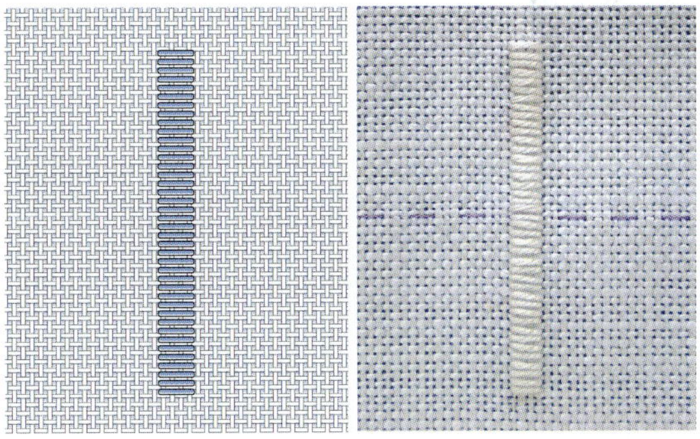

Continue working in the same manner, until there are 41 satin stitches. To finish, run the thread under the back of the stitches, on the back of the fabric.

4 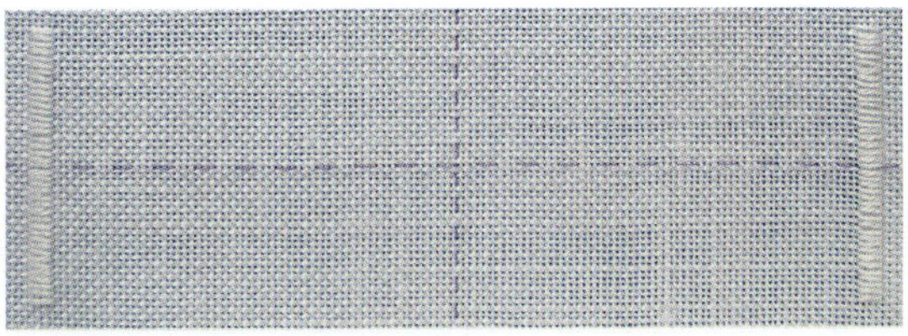

Repeat for the opposite end.

## Cutting and removing threads

**Before stitching the drawn thread work, some of the threads between the satin stitch bars need to be cut and removed.**

1 

At the bottom of the stitching area, the first thread needs to be cut. To cut as close to the satin stitch as possible, without damaging the embroidery threads, slide the point of the scissors underneath the first thread only, returning the point to the surface, to avoid extra accidental cutting. Wiggle the scissors a little to check whether any extra threads are caught on the blade. Carefully cut the thread.

2 Cut the same thread at the far end of the stitching area, just inside the opposite satin stitch bar.

3 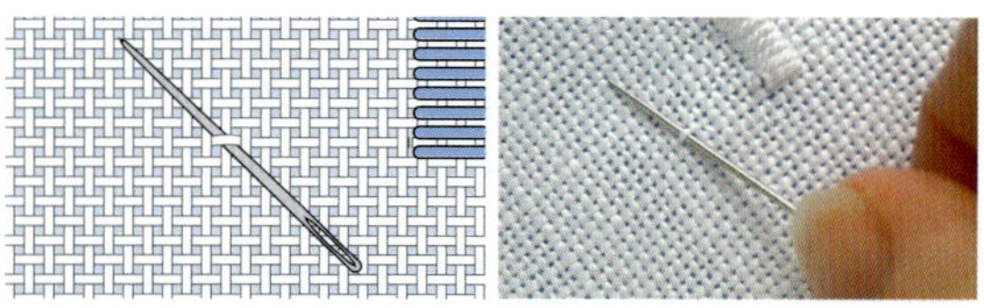

Insert a needle under the thread a short distance (1 cm, 1/4 in) from where it was snipped.

4 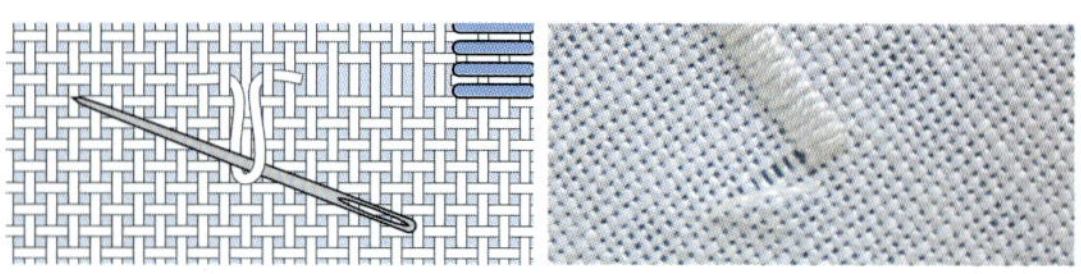

Gently lever the thread end up and out of the fabric.

5 Move further along and repeat, as many times as are necessary to remove the entire section of thread between the two cuts.

## Row 1: hemstitching/prutyk

**Hemstitching is known as 'prutyk' in Ukrainian embroidery. It is worked over bundles of threads, called 'chysnytsia', in the space where the thread has been removed. This project has bundles of three threads, though four is also common. The top and bottom edges of the merezhka band are hemstitched.**

1 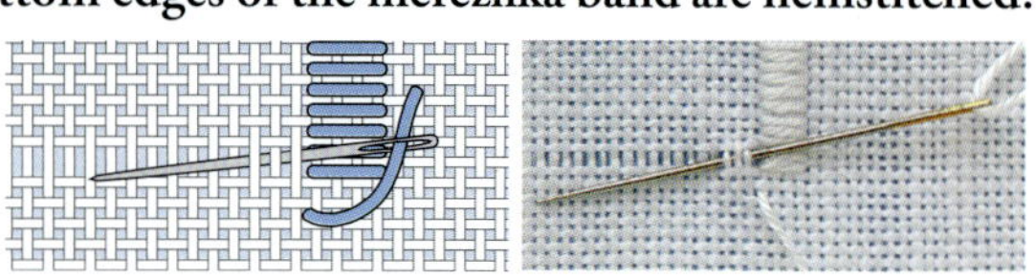

Anchor the thread in the back of the satin stitch. Bring the needle out two threads below the right bottom end of the satin stitching. In the space where the thread has been removed, take the needle under the first three threads next to the satin stitch band.

**!** *Work the row from right to left for right-handed stitchers, and from left to right for left-handed stitchers.*

2 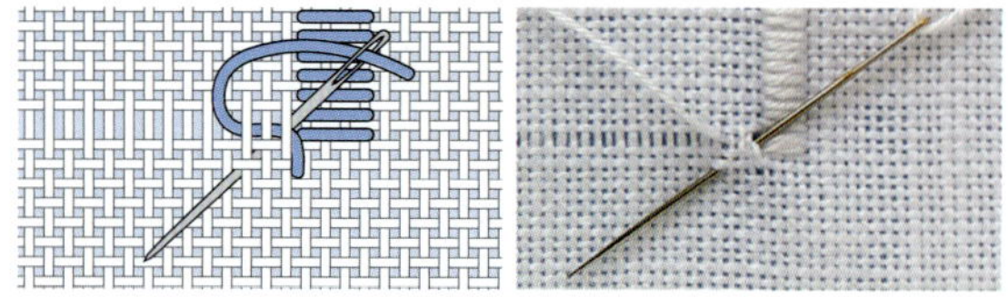

Insert the needle in the space between the satin stitching and the first bundle (chysnytsia) of threads. Bring the needle point out again three threads left and two threads down.

3 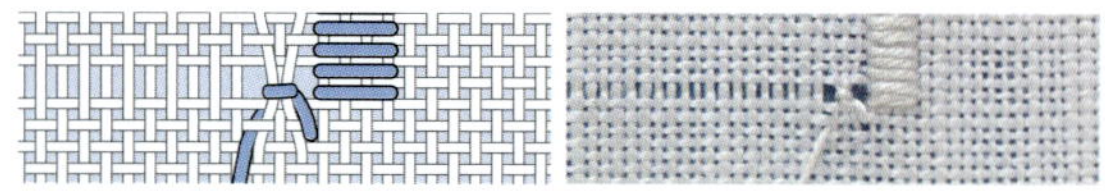

Pull the needle and thread through. Gently pull the thread downwards, to tighten the stitch and bring the fabric threads together.

4 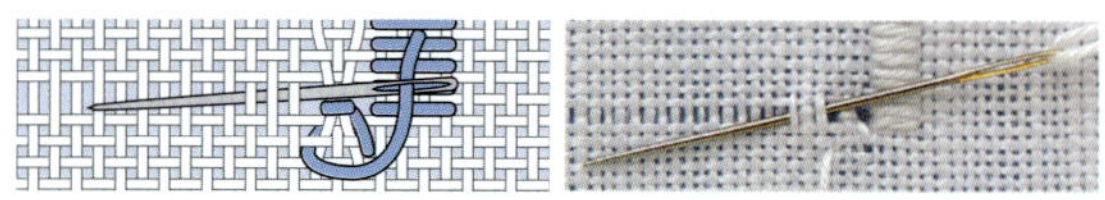

Take the needle under the next three threads.

5 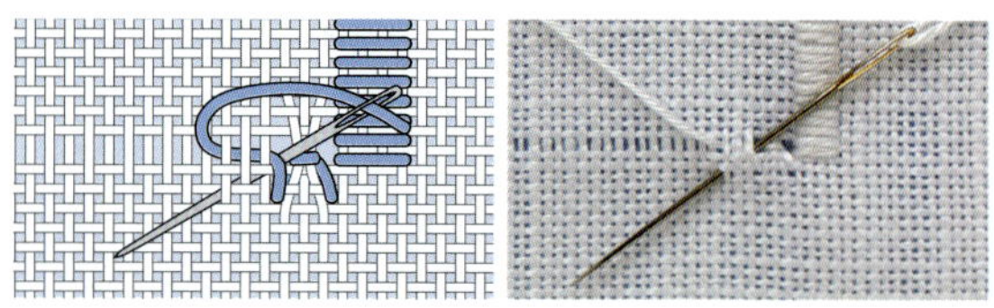

Insert the needle in the space between the first and second chysnytsia. Bring it out again three threads to the left, and two down. Pull the needle through, and gently pull the thread to tighten.

6 

Continue working prutyk along the row, ending at the opposite satin stitch bar. Finish stitching by taking the thread through the back of the hemstitching on the back of the fabric.

## Row 2: layerings

**This section utilises the merezhka technique that is characteristic of the work that comes from Poltava. Known as 'layerings', they consist of three Roman stitches worked over the chysnytsia bundles. Each**

**Roman stitch consists of a thread laid across the bundles, which is then couched between each bundle.**

**During this row more prutyk hemstitching is worked opposite the hemstitching in the first row, thereby creating double prutyk. This is where opposite sides of the row are both hemstitched.**

1

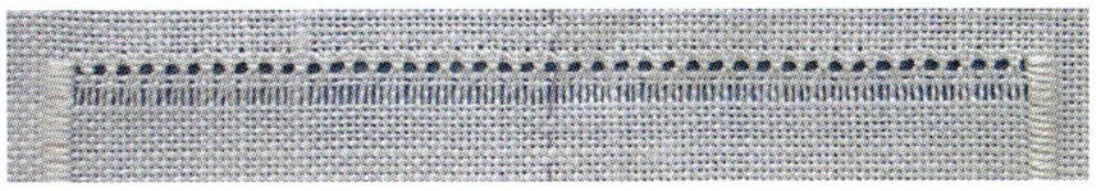

Turn the work 180 degrees, so that the hemstitching is now at the top. Moving down the drawn thread area, leave the next two threads intact, and then cut and remove the following two threads.

- *There are now two rows of removed threads, with the 'double prutyk' row uppermost, a line of woven fabric, and then the first 'layerings' row.*
- *Work the row from right to left for right-handed stitchers, and left to right for left-handed stitchers.*

2

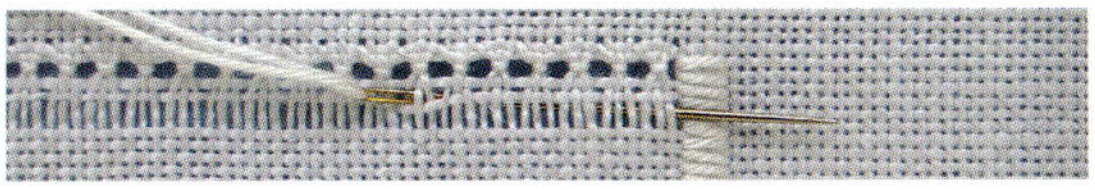

Start with a waste knot: tie a knot in the thread. (The knot will be removed later.) From the front, insert the needle into the woven line about seven chysnytsia groups away from the satin stitch bar. The knot will sit on the front of the fabric. Bring the needle out in the layerings row, next to the satin stitch.

- *While working along the row, ensure this thread is caught into the back of the stitching. Upon reaching the knot, carefully cut it off, and continue stitching.*
- *The first layering is worked over three chysnytsi (plural of chysnytsia). The three double prutyk posts in the previous row are completed first. Following this, the layering is worked over the first three chysnytsi in the current row.*

3

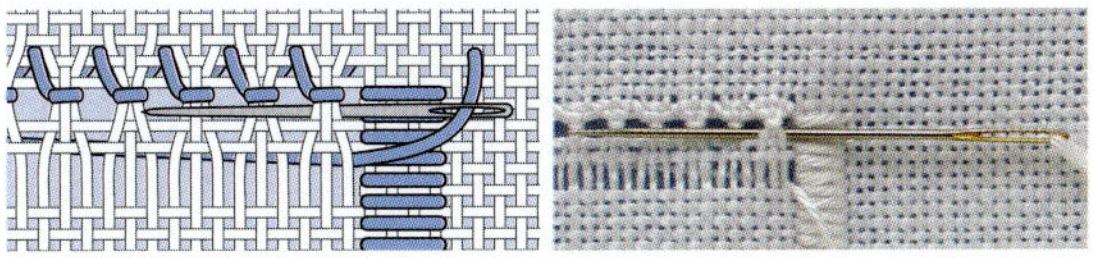

Take the needle under the first chysnytsia in the double prutyk row, above the line of woven fabric.

4

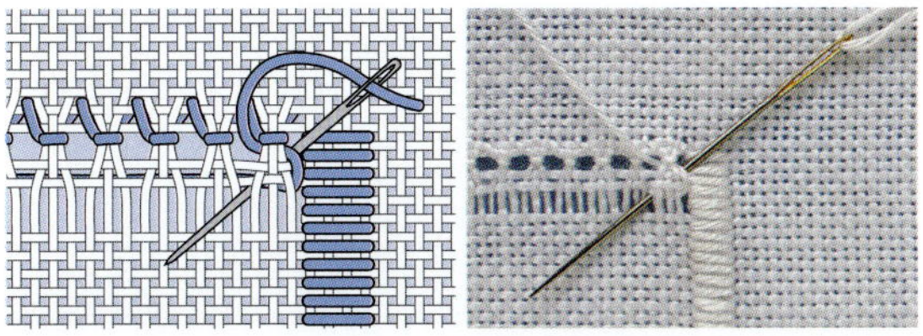

Diagonally insert the needle under the line of woven fabric, from before the first chysnytsia in the double prutyk row, to after the first chysnytsia in the current row of stitching.

5

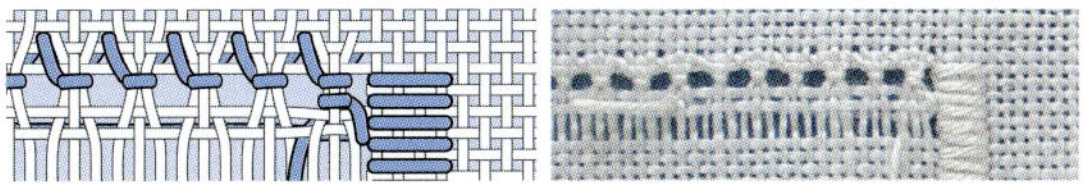

Pull the needle and thread through. Gently pull the thread down to tighten the stitch.

6

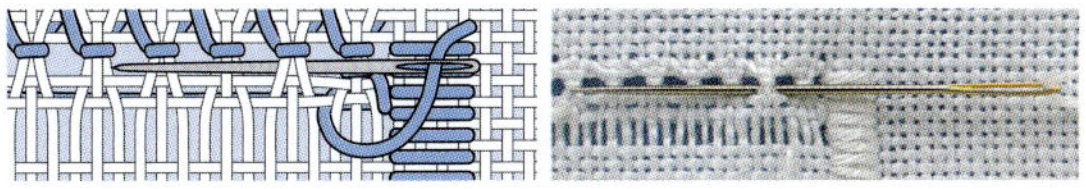

In the double prutyk row, take the needle under the second chysnytsia.

7

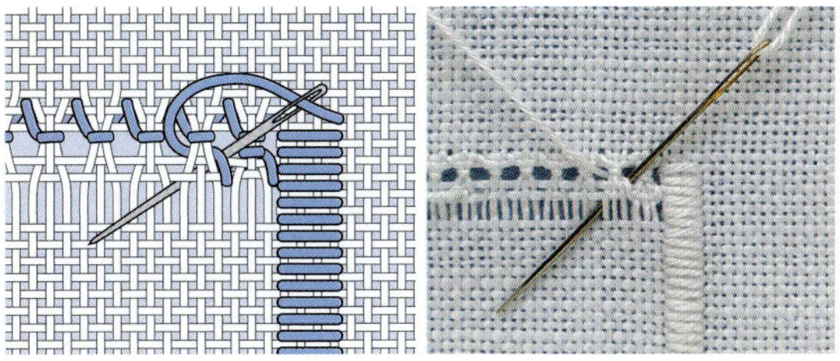

Diagonally insert the needle under the line of woven fabric, from before the second chysnytsia in the double prutyk row, to after the second chysnytsia in the current row of stitching. Pull the needle and thread through, and gently tighten the stitch.

8

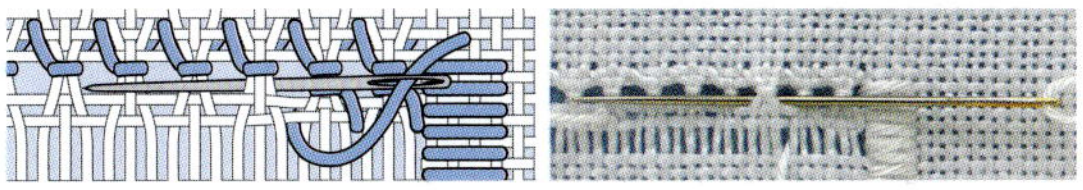

Take the needle under the third chysnytsia in the double prutyk row.

9

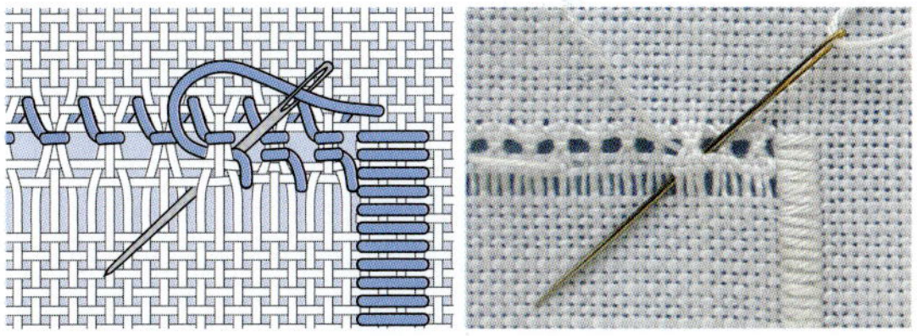

Diagonally insert the needle between the second and third chysnytsi in the prutyk row. The needle emerges between the third and fourth chysnytsi in the first layering row.

10

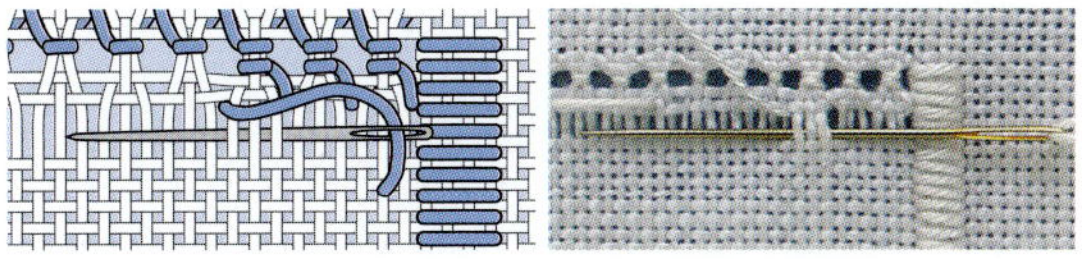

Take the needle under the third chysnytsia.

11

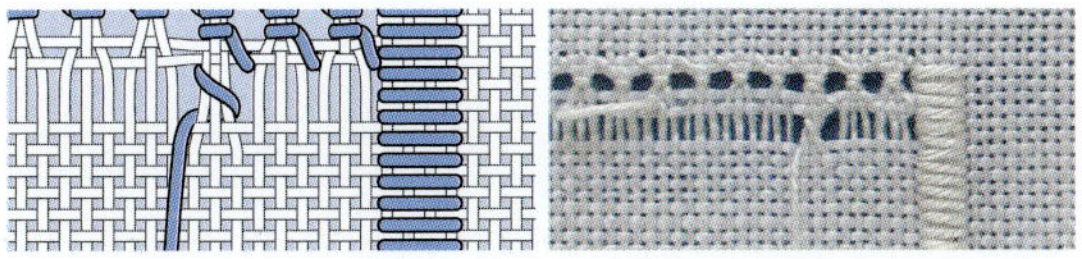

Pull the thread down, to gently tighten the stitch.

12 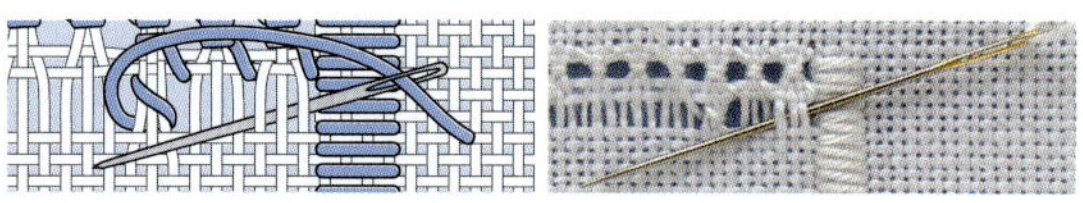

Take the needle under the first chysnytsia.

*This positions the thread correctly for the first Roman stitch. Three Roman stitches, consisting of laid and couched threads, are stacked next to each other, from the bottom up.*

13 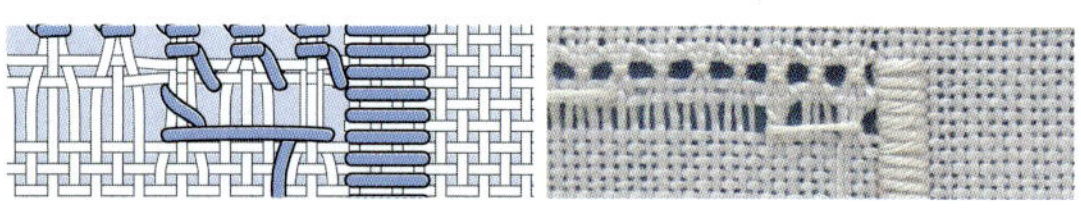

Pull the needle and thread through. Tighten the stitch by pulling the thread downwards until it lies flat on the surface of the fabric.

*This creates the laid thread that will be couched down. It should not be too loose or too tight.*

*The thread must emerge below the laid thread.*

14 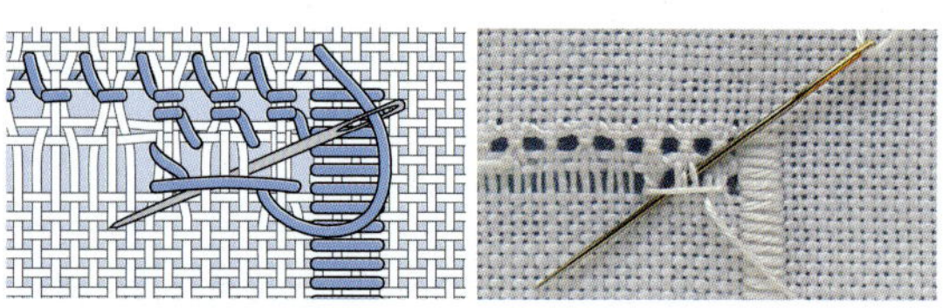

From above the laid thread, insert the needle behind the second chysnytsia. Bring it out below the laid thread.

*This creates a small couching stitch over the laid thread.*

15 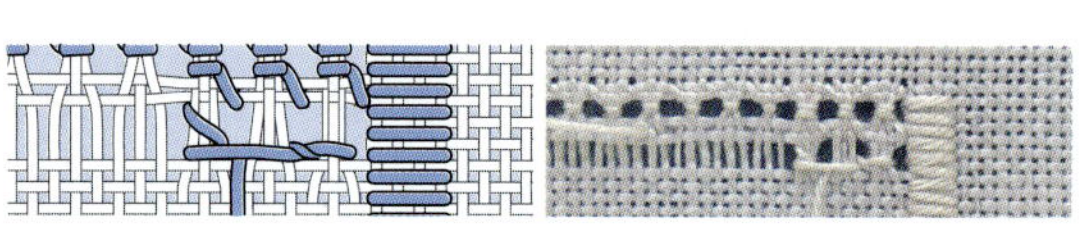

Gently pull the thread down, so that the couching stitch intertwines with the laid stitch.

16 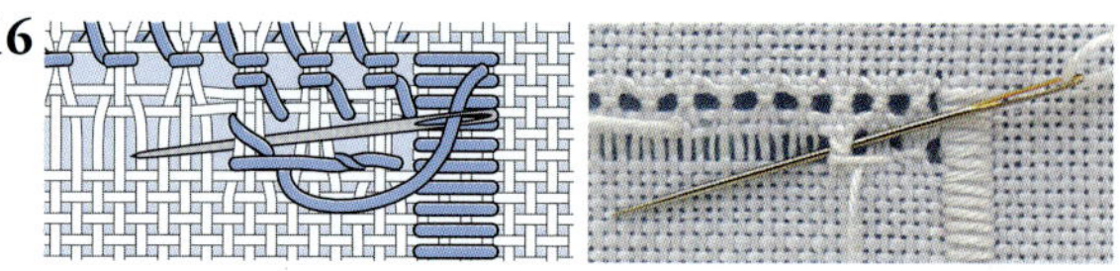

Take the needle under the third chysnytsia, next to the laid stitch.

17 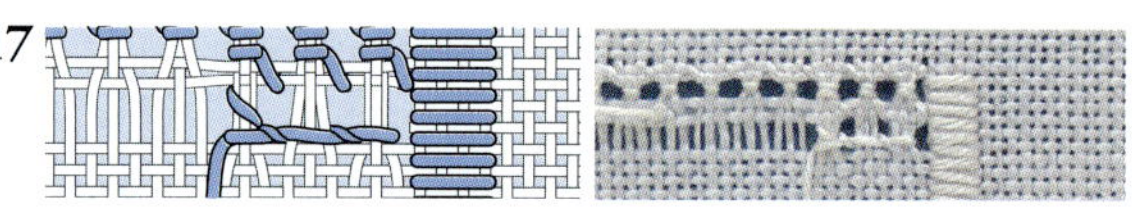

Gently pull the thread down, so that the couching stitch intertwines with the laid stitch.

*This completes the first Roman stitch.*

18 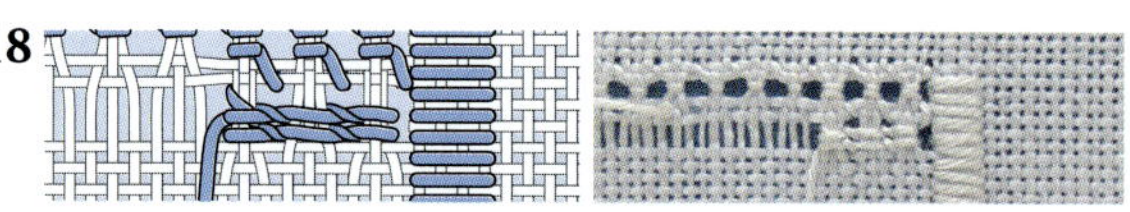

Above the previous stitches, repeat the laying down and couching process to create another Roman stitch.

19 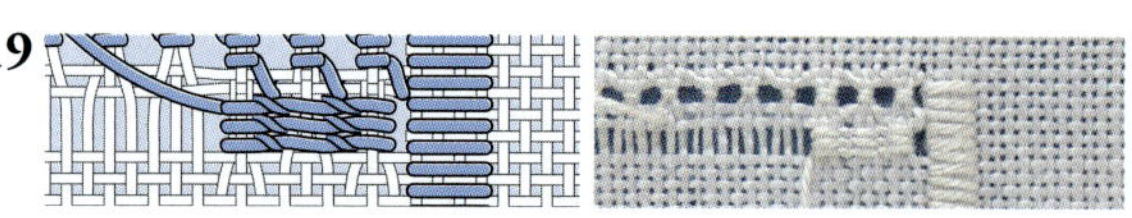

Work a third Roman stitch to complete the layering.

*The completed layering consists of three Roman stitches worked next to each other.*

20 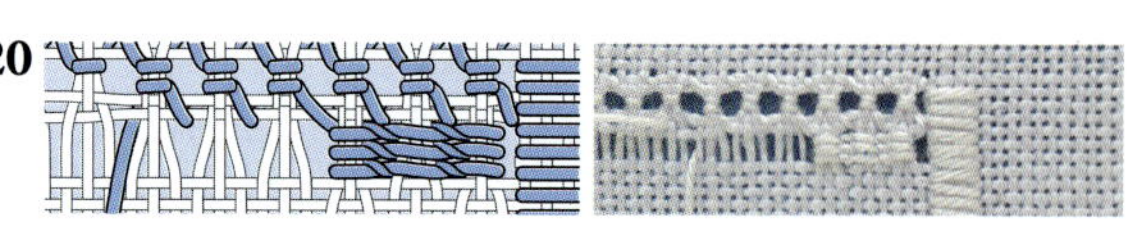

Hemstitch the base of the next three prutyk posts in the previous row.

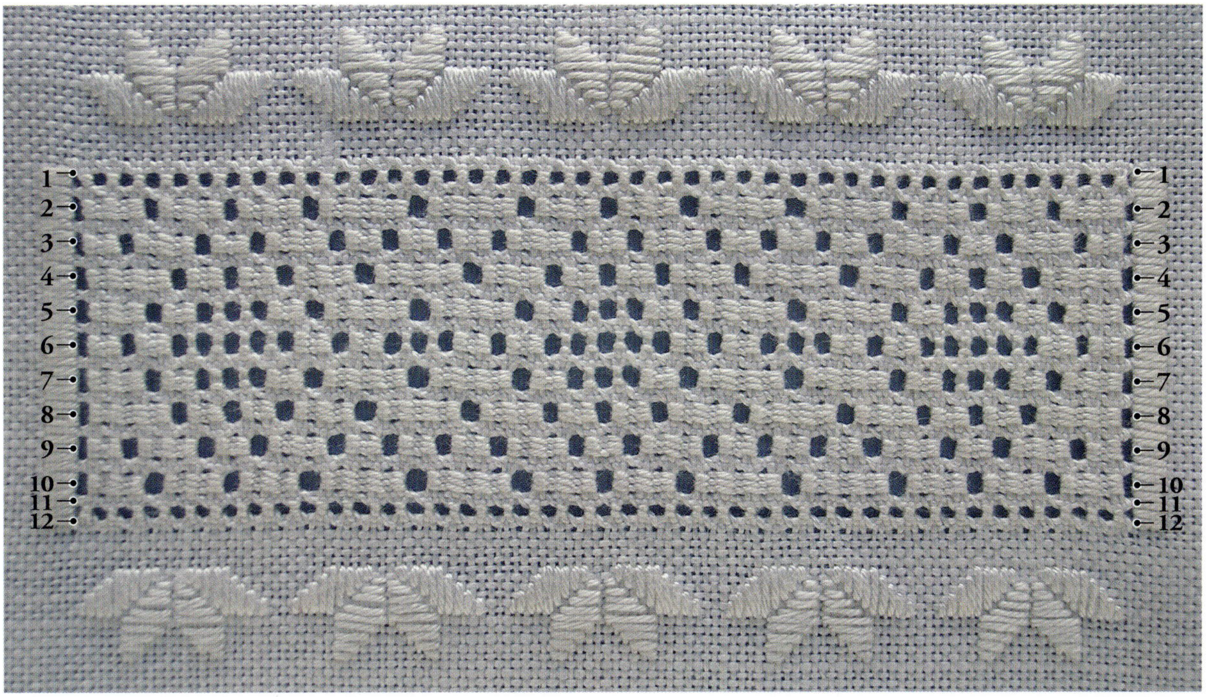


21

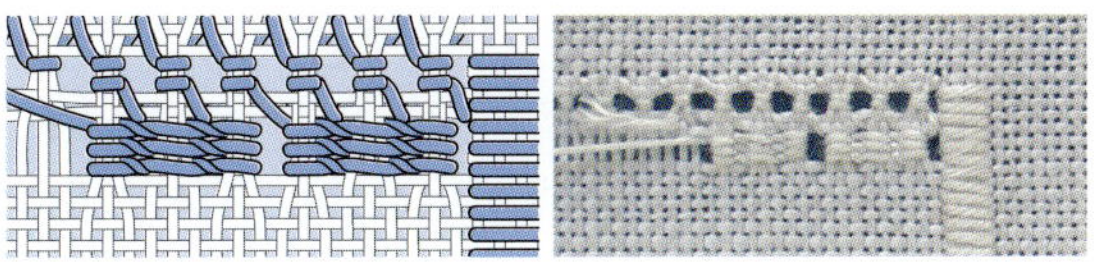

Work Roman stitch layerings over the fourth, fifth and sixth chysnytsi, as per the chart.

22

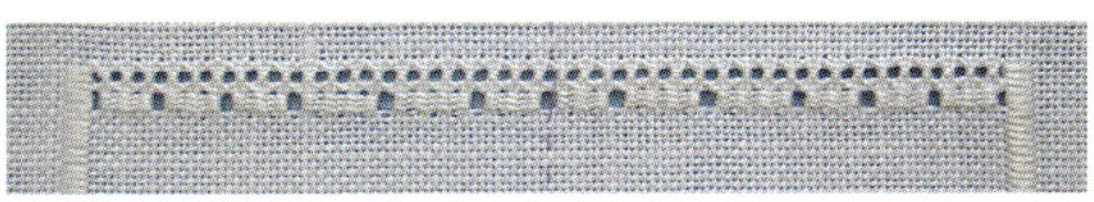

Continue the process of working prutyk and layerings for the remainder of the row, following the pattern chart. To finish the thread, on the back of the fabric, take the needle under the stitching.

- *Multiple layering rows can be worked with a number of threads and needles underway at once. This assists some stitchers in making sure the pattern is correct. However, the threads can easily become entangled.*
- *Rows must be stitched right to left (or vice versa for left-handed stitchers). They cannot be started halfway along and then worked back to each end, as the stitching would look different on the part that is worked left to right.*
- *See page 26 for how to finish an old thread and start a new one during a row.*

## Row 3: layerings

**In this row a whip stitch is used to move along the woven row, instead of the prutyk hemstitching as used in the previous row.**

1 Moving down the drawn thread area, leave the next two threads intact, and cut and remove the following two.

2

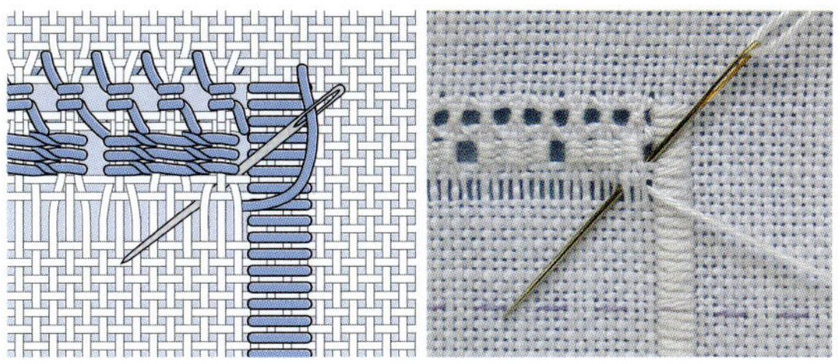

Diagonally take the needle under the woven section, from before the first chysnytsia in the previous row to after the first chysnytsia in the current row. Gently tighten the stitch.

- *This creates a small whip stitch over the woven section.*

3

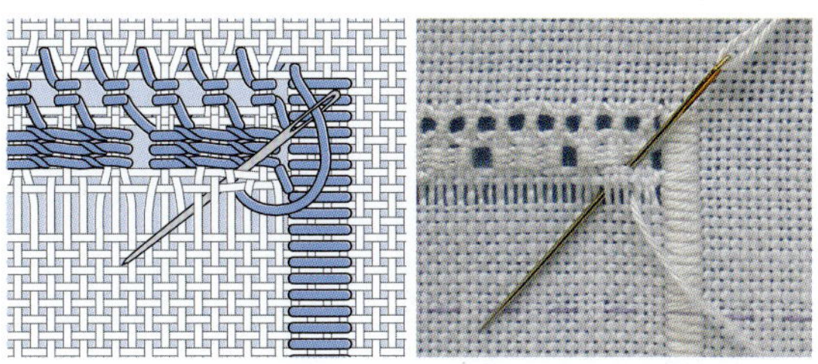

Insert the needle above the second woven row, between the first and second chysnytsi. Bring the needle out again in the second layering row, between the second and third chysnytsi.

4

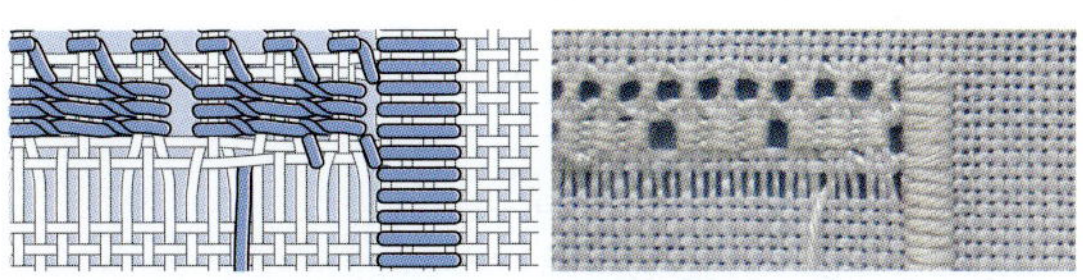

Pull the needle and thread through.

- *This time, according to the chart, the layering is worked over only two chysnytsi.*

5
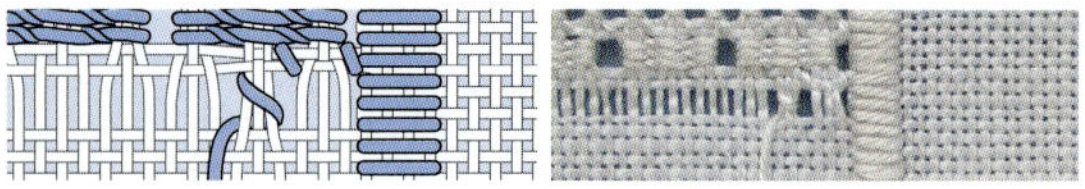

Take the needle under the second chysnytsia and gently tighten the stitch.

6
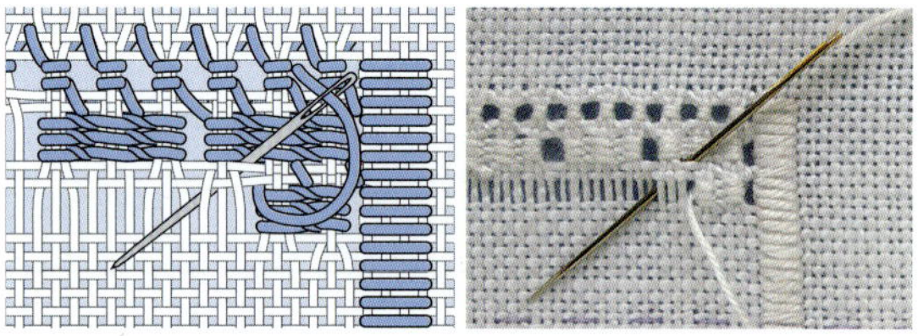

Work three Roman stitches over the two chysnytsi, to complete the first set of layerings. Work a whip stitch over the woven section so as to reach the position for the next layerings.

7

Continue, working the row according to the chart.

## Row 4: layerings

1 Moving down, leave the next two threads intact, and cut and remove the following two.

2

Work the row according to the pattern chart.

## Row 5: layerings with prutyk

**When the pattern indicates a single chysnytsia, this is worked as a double prutyk. The top of the double prutyk is worked in one row, with the bottom of the double prutyk being worked in the next row.**

1
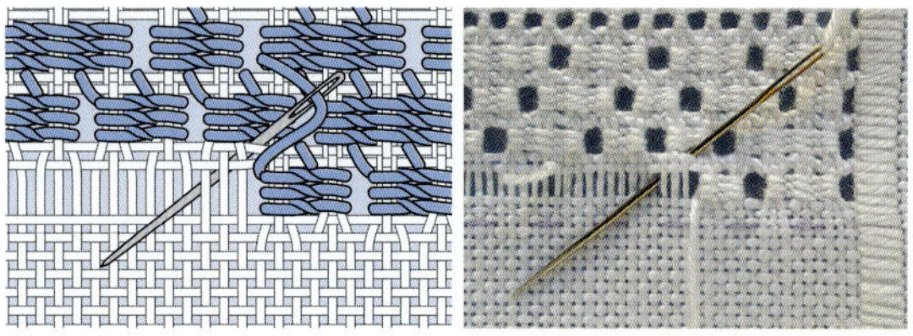

Work the first two layerings according to the chart. Work the next whip stitch over the woven section.

2
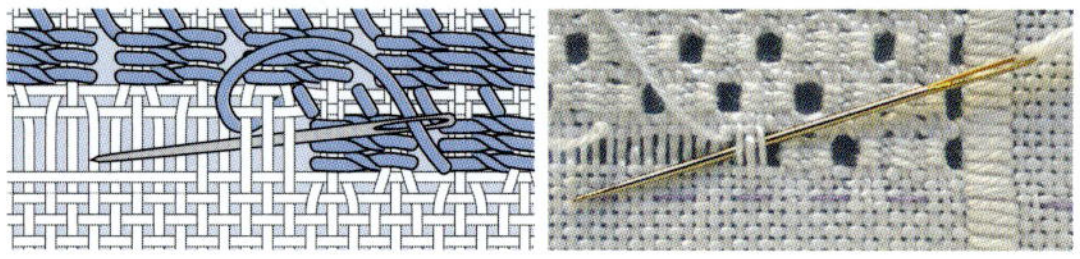

Take the needle under the sixth chysnytsia.

*This creates the top of the first double prutyk within the row of layerings.*

3
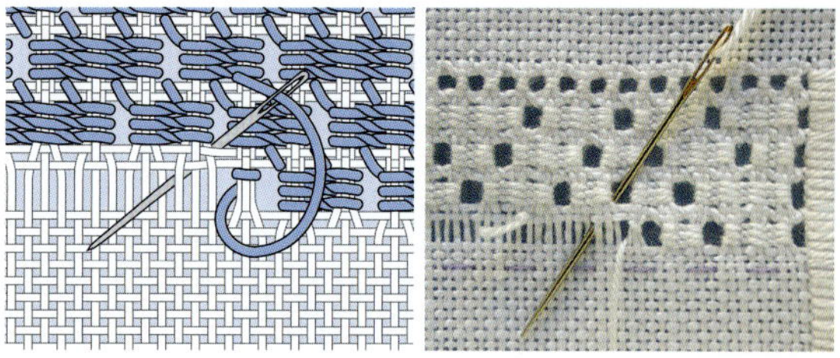

Work the next whip stitch over the woven section.

4
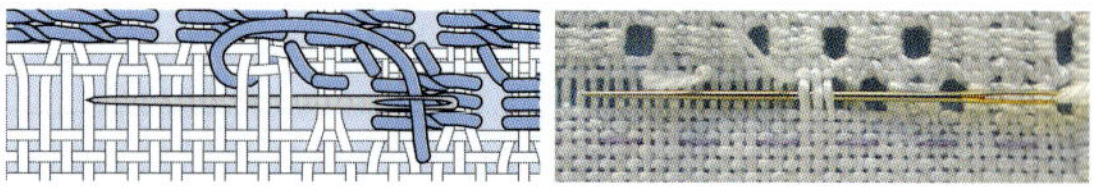

Take the needle under the seventh chysnytsia.

5

Work the next whip stitch over the woven section.

6

Work the remainder of the row according to the pattern chart, working layerings and the tops of double prutyk posts as required.

## Row 6: layerings with prutyk

**In this row, the prutyk posts from the previous row are completed, in addition to working the layerings and double prutyk for this row.**

1 Following the pattern chart, work the first two layerings and the top of a double prutyk post.

2
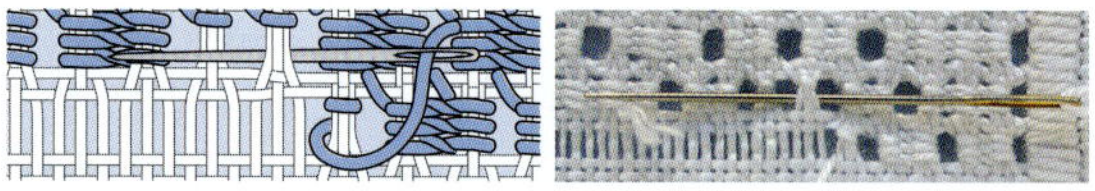

To work the bottom of the double prutyk post in the previous row, take the needle under the first unfinished double prutyk in the row above.

3
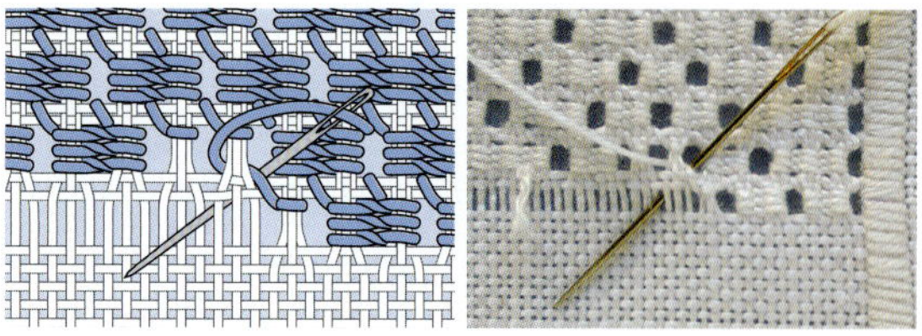

Diagonally take the needle under the woven section from before the prutyk post in the first row, to after the corresponding chysnytsia in the current row.

4 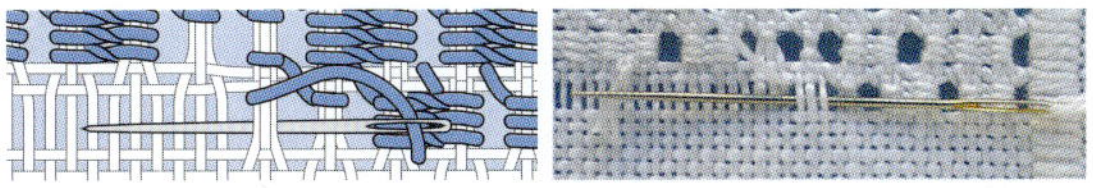

Work a prutyk in the current row.

5 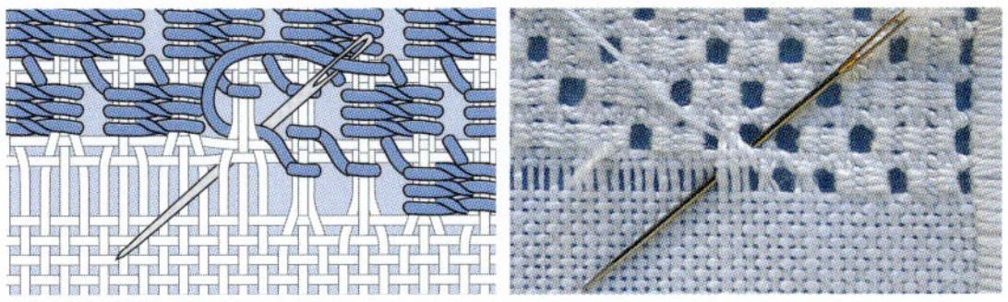

Complete the bottom of the next unfinished double prutyk in the previous row.

6 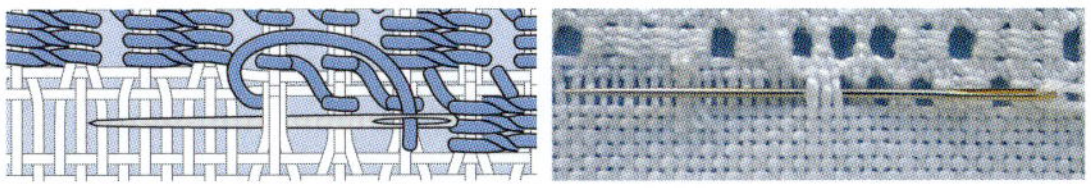

Work a prutyk in the current row.

7 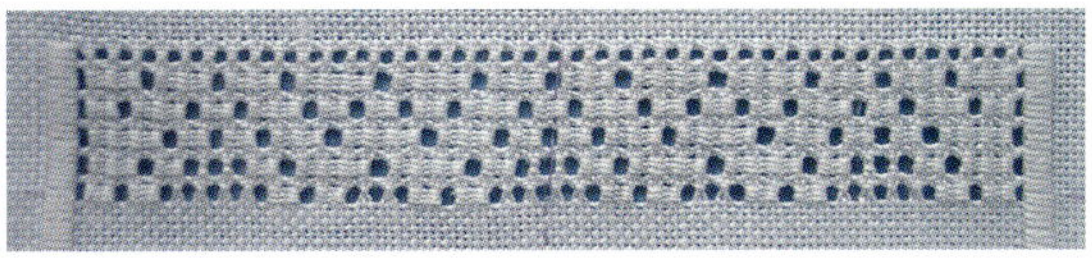

Following the chart, work the remainder of the row, working layerings and prutyk, and completing the double prutyk posts in the previous row.

## Rows 7–10

1 

Work row 7 according to the chart.

2 

Work row 8 according to the chart.

3 

Work row 9 according to the chart.

4 

Work row 10 according to the chart.

## Row 11: double prutyk

**1** Leave two threads, then remove one thread only (not two, as in previous rows).

**2** Work prutyk over each chysnytsia in the row.

## Row 12: double prutyk

**1** Turn the work 180 degrees.

2 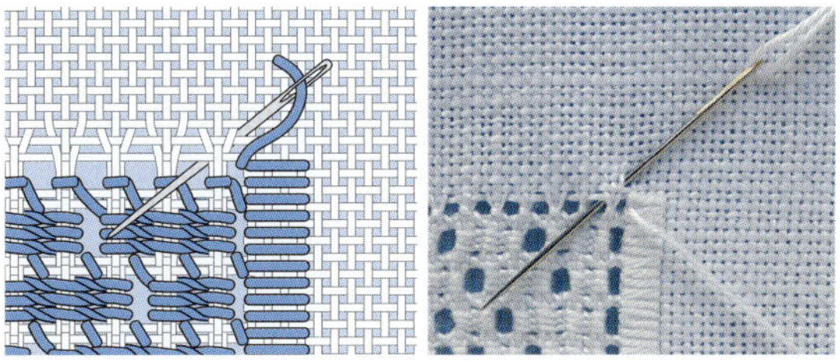

Bring the needle out in the space before the first chysnytsia. Count two threads up, and insert the needle. Bring the needle out in the space between the first and second chysnytsi.

3 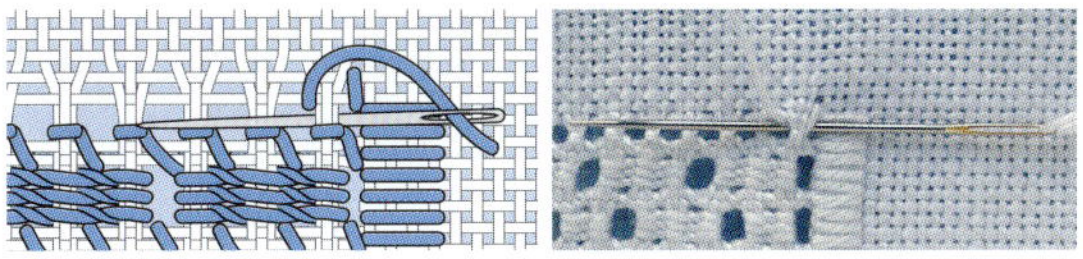

Take the needle under the first chysnytsia.

4 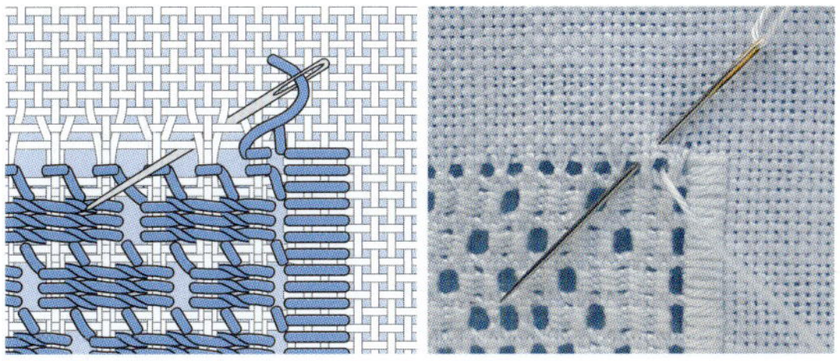

Count two threads up, and insert the needle. Bring it out between the second and third chysnytsi.

5 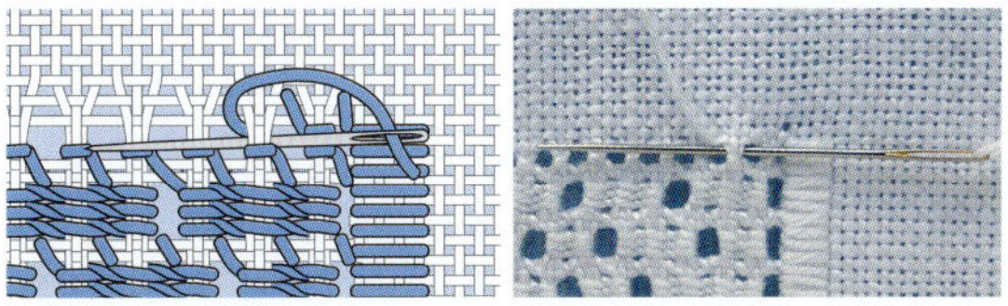

Take the needle under the second chysnytsia.

6 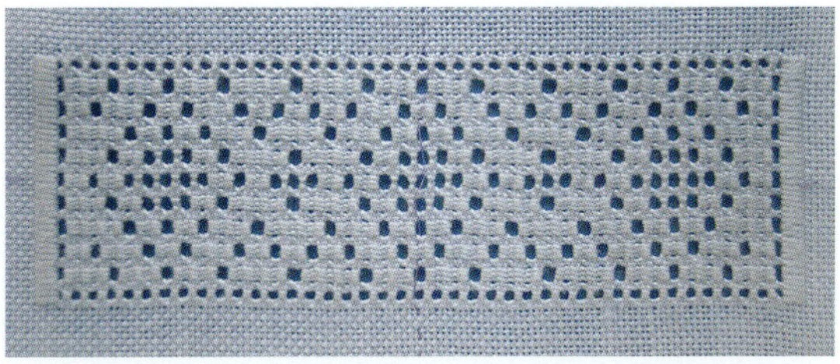

Complete the row following the same sequence.

## Satin stitch flower motifs

**The satin stitch flower motifs are half of eight-pointed satin stitch star motifs. Worked using satin stitch, as for the satin stitch bands, position the stitches for each 'petal' according to the chart.**

1 Turn the fabric 90 degrees. At the centre bottom of the merezhka band, count four threads towards the edge of the fabric, along the tacking. Count two threads down, and bring the needle out.

2 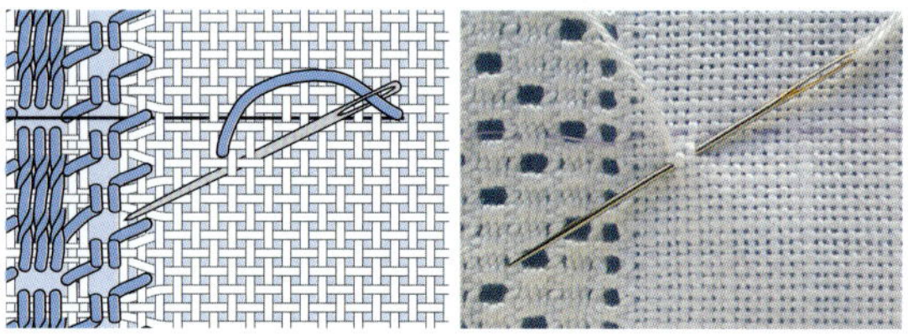

Insert the needle two threads to the right, bring it out one thread lower than where it previously emerged.

3 Pull the needle and thread through, so that the thread lies flat against the fabric, not too tight or too loose.

4 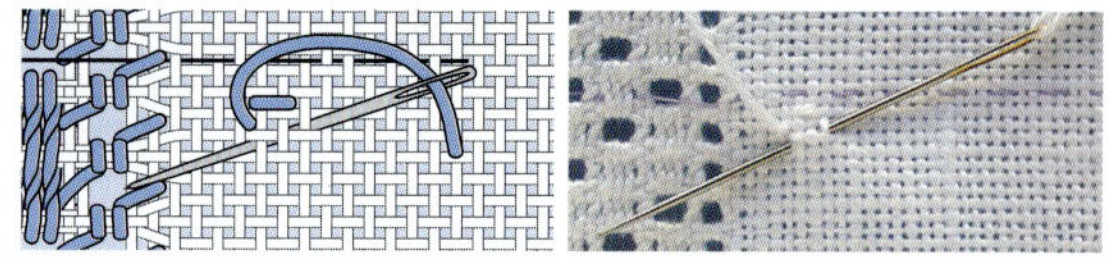

Insert the needle three threads to the right, and bring it out one thread below where it previously emerged.

5 

Continue, following the chart to complete the first petal. On the reverse, run the thread under the stitches, back to the centre of the flower motif.

6 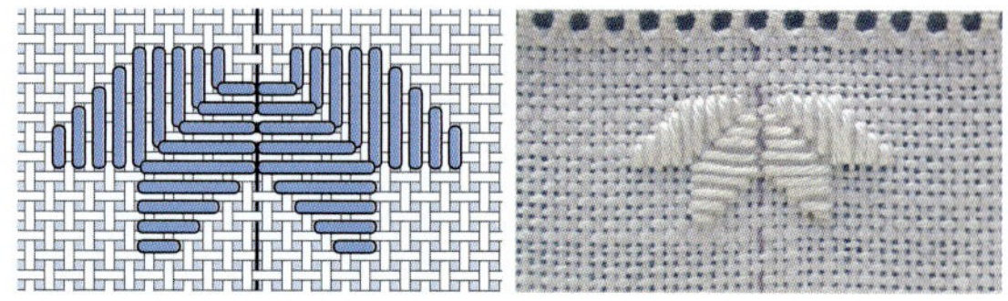

Complete the remainder of the flower motifs according to the pattern chart.

### WHAT WENT WRONG? AVOIDING AND FIXING MISTAKES

#### Poor tension

Too loose The gaps between the layerings close up and the pattern becomes less pronounced. The couching stitches form ridges down the layerings rather than 'melting in'. Gently pull each stitch to tighten as you work. This can take courage, so be bold!

Too tight This causes pulling at the edges of the merezhka. If you have to undo any mistakes, on restitching you may find that the tension becomes too tight as the threads will have already been pulled together. Slacken your tension a little. Do not tighten the laid threads so much that they pull in the sides of the chysnytsi. They should lay flat over the chysnytsi only.

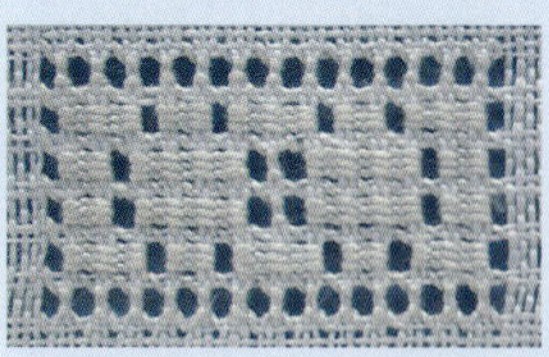

Good tension There is adequate space between each layering. The couching stitches are not raised above the laid stitches. There is no puckering at the sides of the merezhka band.

#### Bottom stitches of double prutyk missing

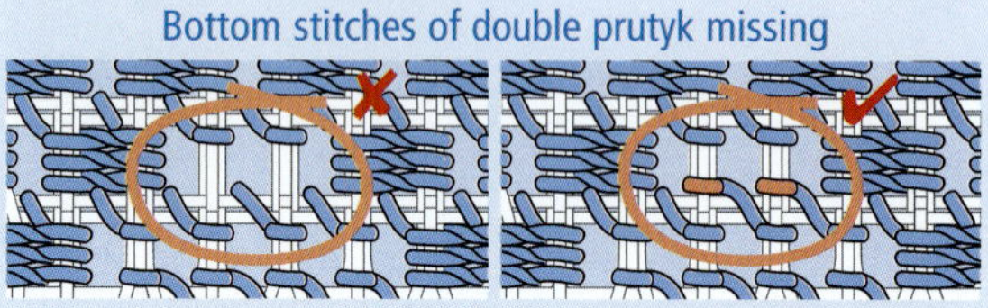

It is very easy to accidentally skip the bottom end of a prutyk post, as it is worked in the row after the rest of the current row. Always remember to finish the prutyk post during the next row.

#### Couching stitches which don't all lie the same way

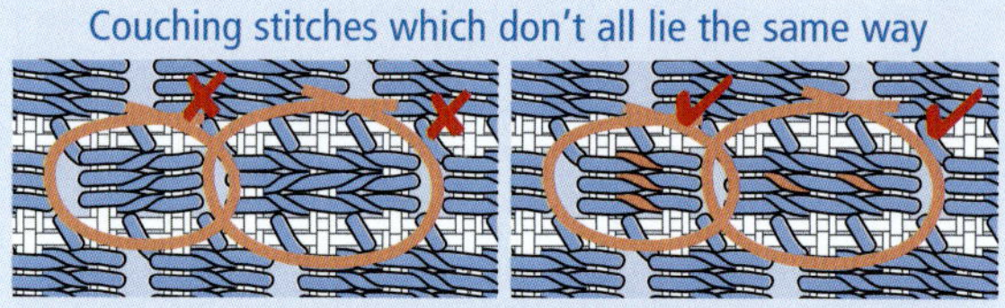

All the couching stitches should cross the laid threads the same way. They should also lie the same way as the whip stitches.

#### Incorrect placement of whip stitches

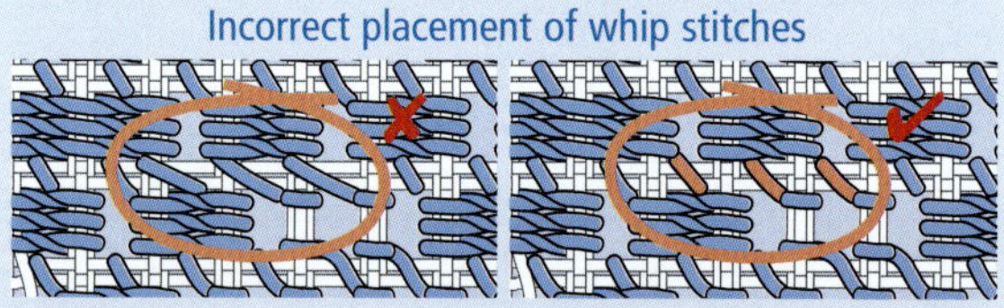

The whip stitches that are used to move along the woven section of the row must pass between chysnytsi, and not over the front of them as shown in the left diagram.

#### Whip stitches missing

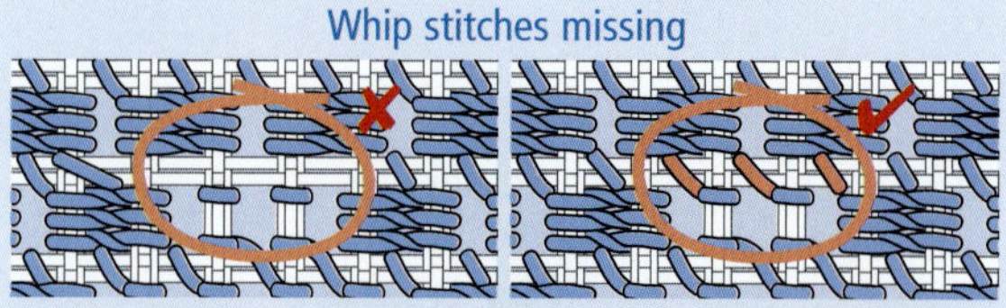

Make sure the whip stitches are in place for moving along the line. Between each chysnytsia, there should always be a whip stitch crossing the adjacent woven section.

#### Thread untwisted or too twisted

Make sure your thread doesn't become untwisted or too twisted as you stitch. If it does, let the needle drop and let it untwist or retwist back to its natural state. You could also regularly make a small twist (or untwist) between each stitch so that it doesn't build up.

CHAPTER 3

# Learning sampler 2

## Small scale merezhka

Small scale Merezhka Poltavska was historically used on shirts. It is worked on finer fabric and spanning fewer threads than the large scale technique. Two threads are removed for each large scale merezhka row, with only one for small scale. While large scale single chysnytsi are worked as double prutyk, small scale ones are worked as a double wrap prutyk as part of the subsequent row.

**SIZE** 2.5 x 10 cm (1 x 4 in)

**MATERIALS REQUIRED**

- 25 x 30 cm (10 x 12 in) 32 count linen, white
- 23 m (25 yd) Thin thread, white (see 'Compatibility', p7)
- No 24 tapestry needle

## Preparing the stitching area

**An alternative to using the counted tacking centre guides as described in Chapter 2, is to define the edges of the drawn thread area with tacking.**

1 Fold the fabric in half both ways. Where the fold lines cross each other is the centre of the fabric. Mark this point with a pin.

2

From the pin, on the longer fold, carefully count out 61 threads out to one side. Tack a line perpendicular to the fold at this point.

3

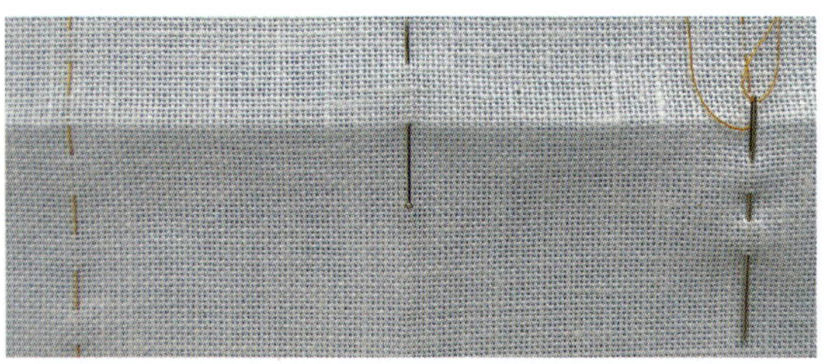

On the same fold, carefully count out 62 threads from the pin, to the opposite side. Tack a line parallel to the first one at this point.

4

On the shorter fold, carefully count 12 threads from the pin, out to one side. Tack a line across the longer dimension at this point.

5

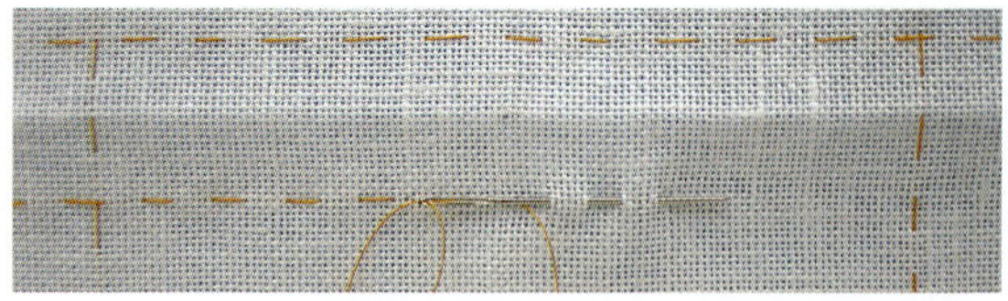

On the same fold, from the pin, carefully count 13 threads to the opposite side. Tack a line across the fabric, parallel to the previous one.

*The drawn thread area is bounded by the tacked guides.*

## Roman stitch end bars

**The ends of this band are worked in Roman stitch – the same stitch that is used for the merezhka layerings.**

1

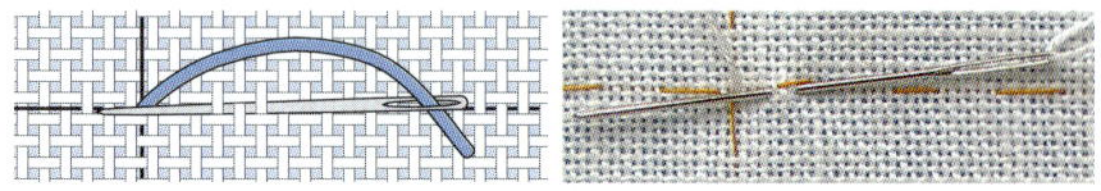

Thread a length of Thin thread. Bring the needle out at the top left of the stitching area. Insert it six threads to the right, bringing it out again below the laid thread, three threads to the left. Pull the needle and thread through.

*The beginning of the thread can be caught in the back of the stitching as it progresses, or alternatively left hanging and threaded into the back at the completion of the bar.*

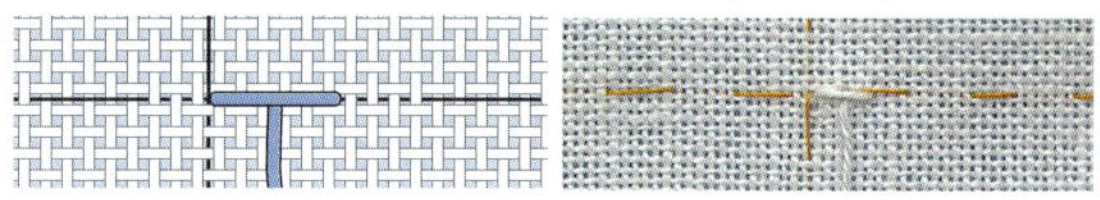

*The thread will sit flat against the fabric, thus creating the laid thread.*

2

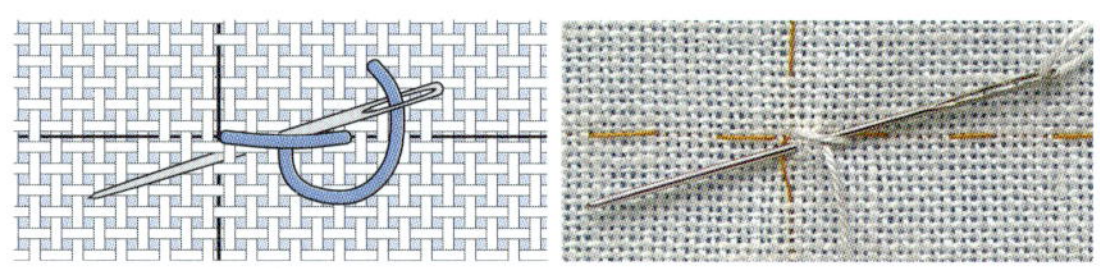

Insert the needle in the same fabric hole, on the opposite side of the laid thread. Bring the needle out one thread below where the previous Roman stitch began.

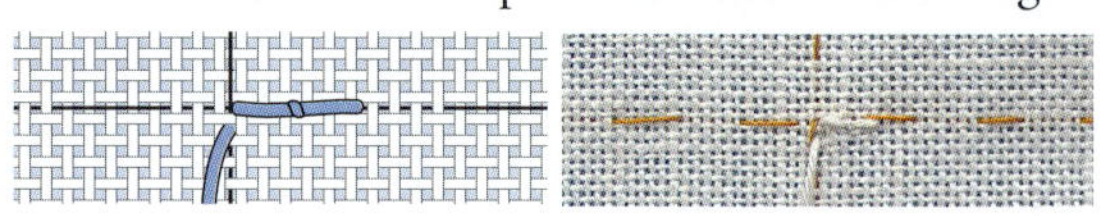

*This creates a small couching stitch over the laid thread.*

3

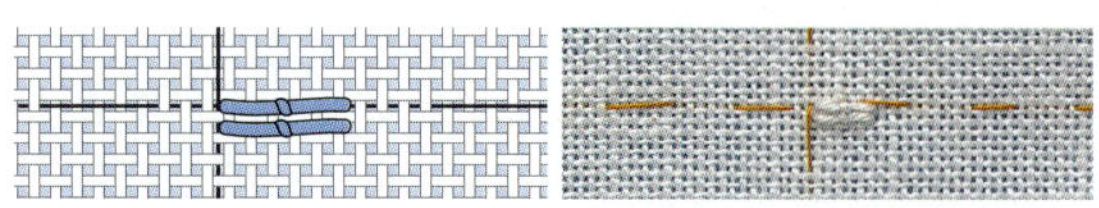

Work another Roman stitch as a twin for the first one.

4

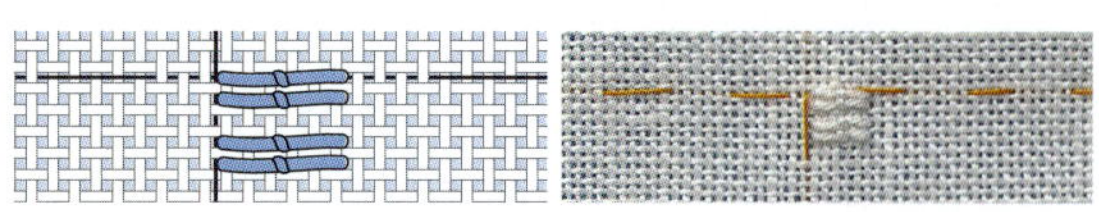

Following the chart, leave two threads then work another pair of Roman stitches.

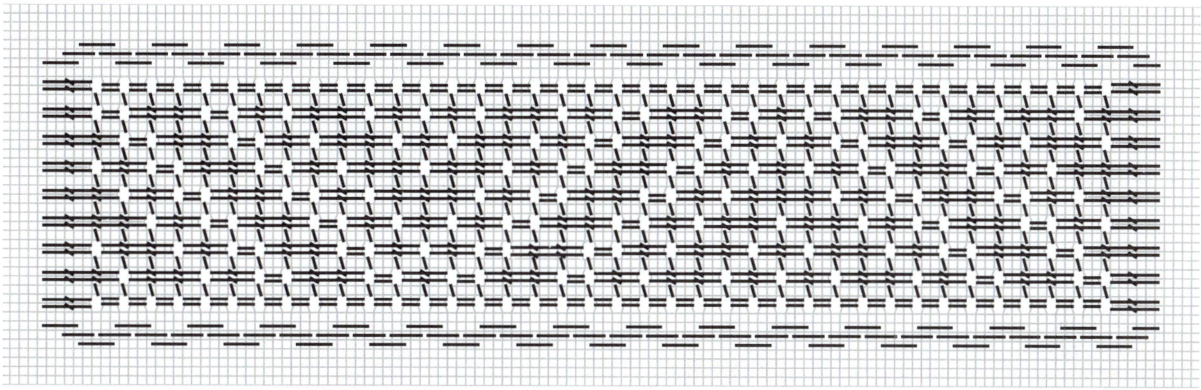

5

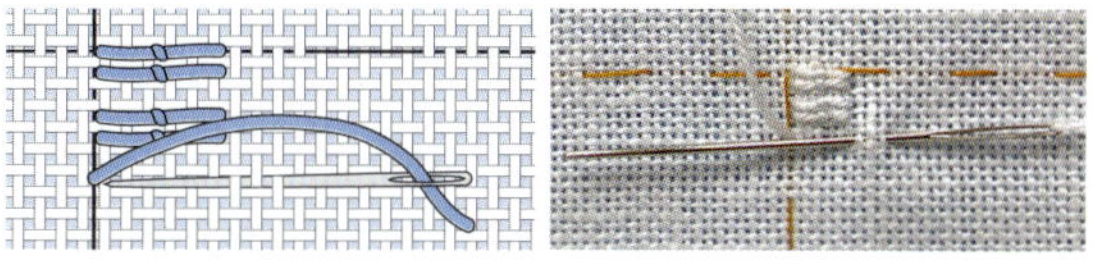

Moving down, skip two threads, then work a laid stitch across nine threads. Bring the needle out three threads to the left, below the laid stitch.

6

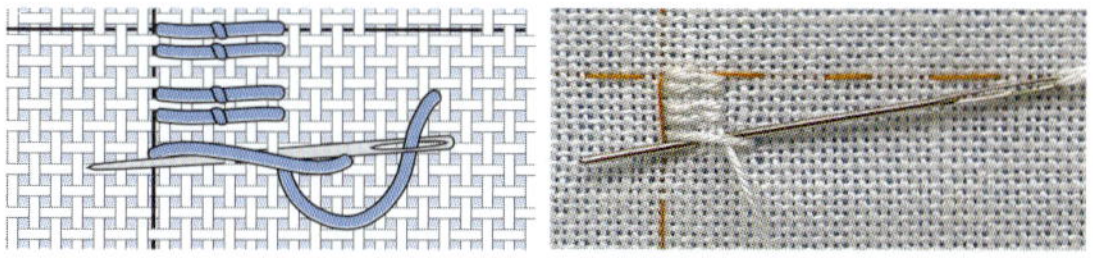

Insert the needle above the laid thread in the same hole, and bring the needle out three threads further to the left, below the laid thread.

7

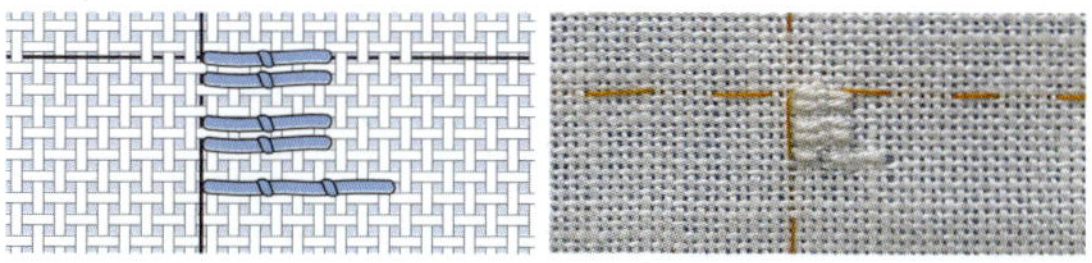

Work another couching stitch over the laid thread to finish the Roman stitch.

8

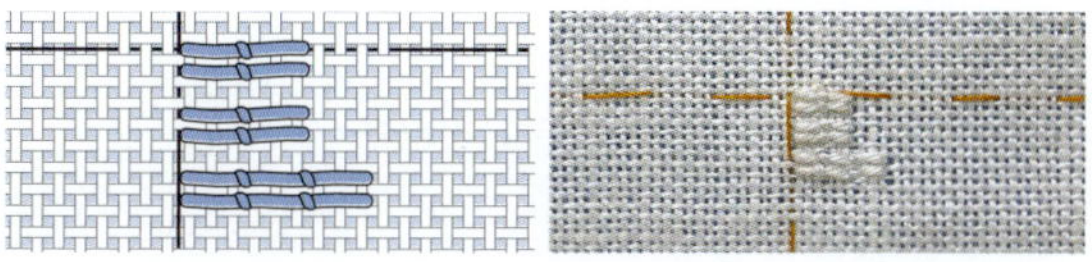

Work another Roman stitch as twin to the previous one, one thread below.

9

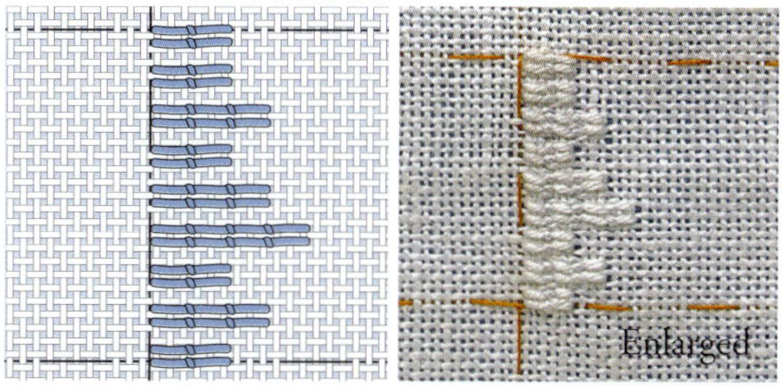


Continue following the pattern, creating twin Roman stitches of the required lengths to complete the end bar.

❶ *Finish the thread by taking it through the back of the stitching, on the reverse of the fabric.*

10

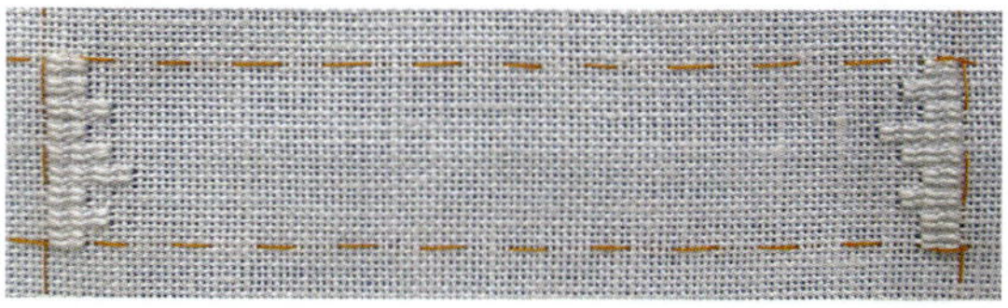

Following the pattern, create another Roman stitch end bar at the other end of the drawn thread area.

## Cutting and removing threads

**Between the Roman stitch bars, the threads need to be cut and removed in order to work the merezhka stitching. In this small scale technique, single threads are removed, rather than the pairs that are removed in the large scale technique.**

1

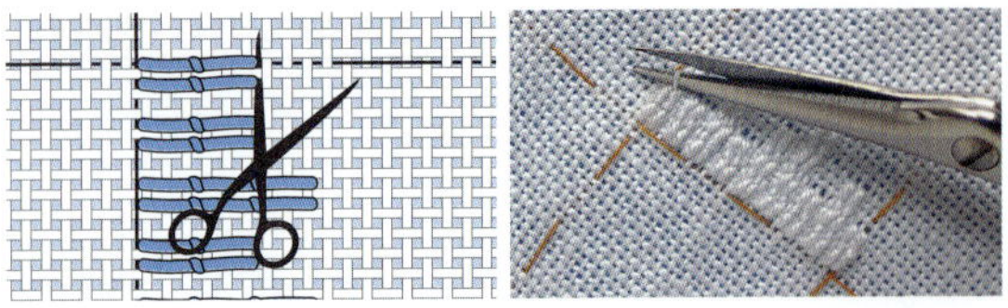

A thread emerges from between the top left Roman stitch pair. Insert the scissor point under this thread, adjacent to the stitches. Ensure that none of the stitching thread is caught on the blade and then carefully cut.

2

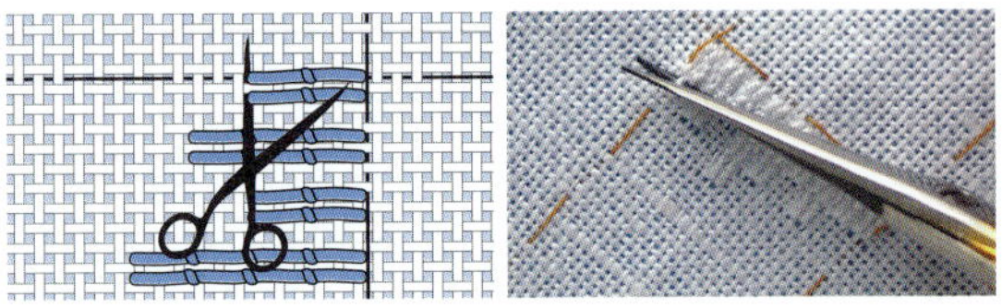

Repeat at the other end of the stitching area.

3

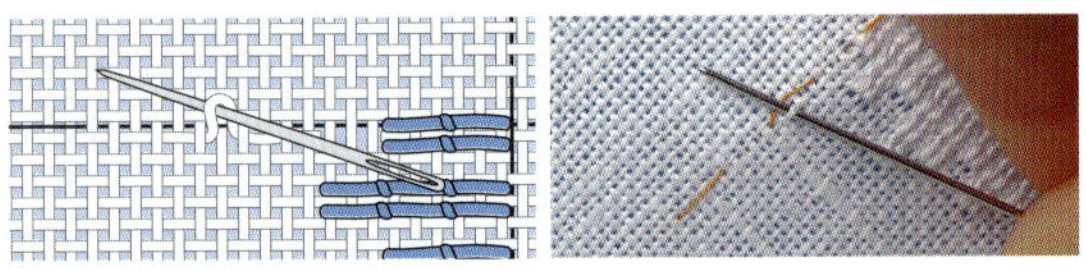

Insert a needle under the thread, close to one of the cuts. Gently lever it upwards so that the end comes out of the fabric. Move further along and repeat, so that the entire cut section is removed.

4

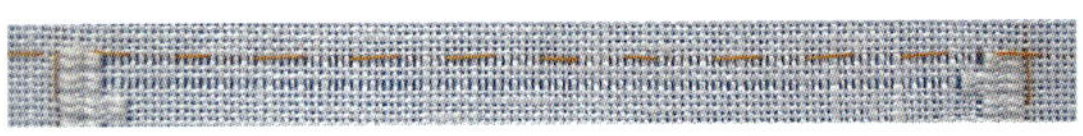

Move down two threads and repeat for the second Roman stitch pair.

## Rows 1 & 2: prutyk and layerings

**In the small scale technique, unlike the large scale variation, there is no hemstitching at the top and bottom of the band. Instead, the prutyk of Row 1 is worked with a double wrap while working the first row of layerings (Row 2).**

**Layerings are worked over bundles of three threads, with only two Roman stitches per layering. Stitching is worked from right to left (vice versa for left-handers).**

1

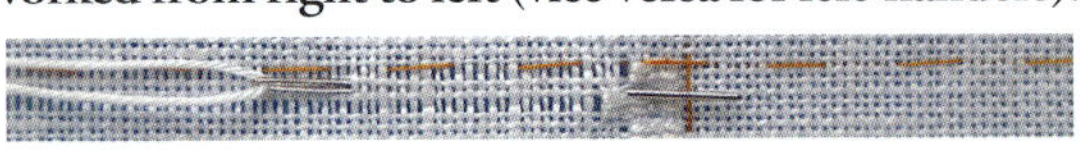

Use a waste knot to begin. Bring the needle out two threads down from the Roman stitches in Row 1.

*This will be from the same hole as the couching part of the Roman stitch in Row 2.*

2

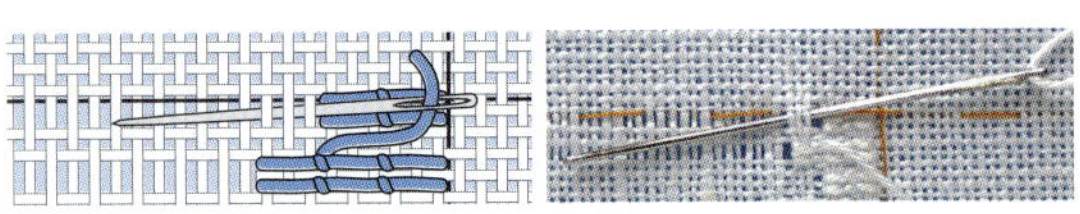

Take the needle under the first three threads (chysnytsia) in Row 1. Gently tighten the stitch.

3

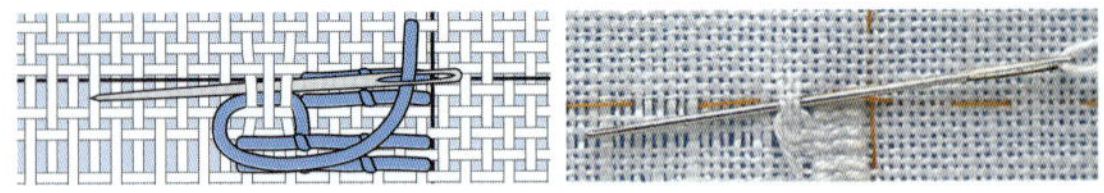

Take the needle under the first chysnytsia again and gently tighten the stitch.

4

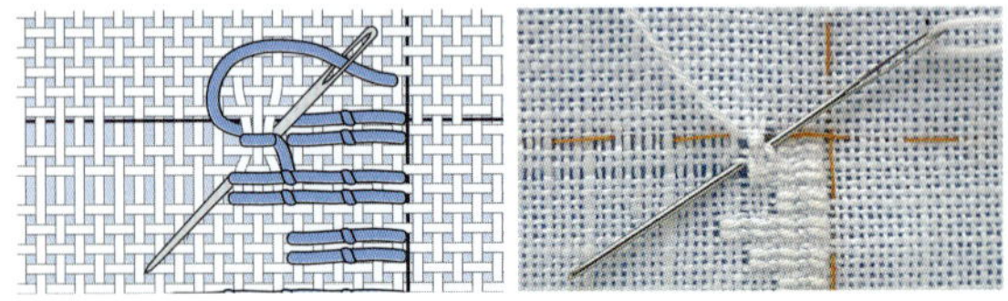

Insert the needle before the first chysnytsia in Row 1, bringing it out in Row 2, next to the Roman stitches.

5

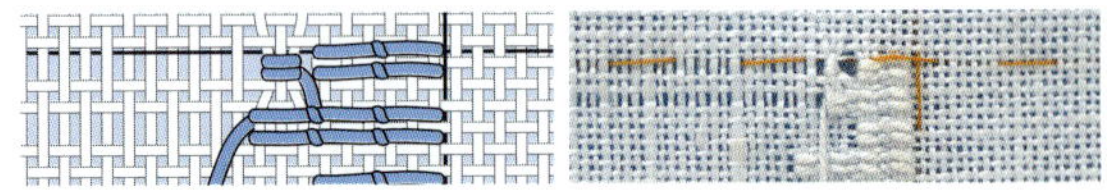

Gently tighten the stitch.

*This creates the first double wrap prutyk in Row 1.*

6

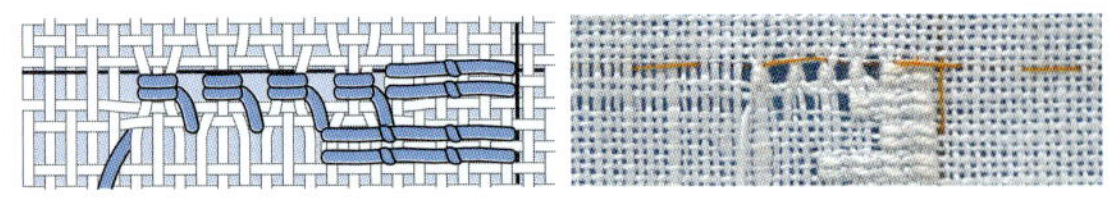

Work double wrap prutyk in the same way, for the next three chysnytsi in Row 1.

7

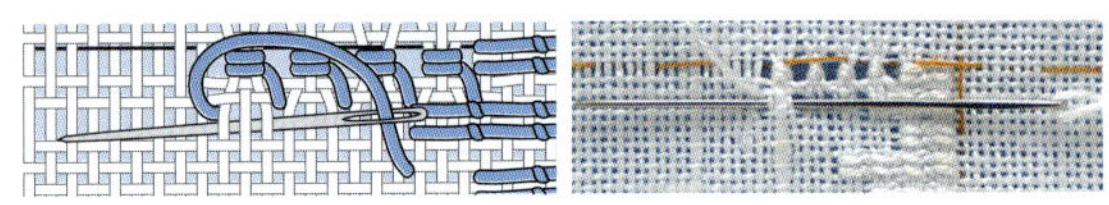

Take the needle under the third chysnytsia in Row 2.

8

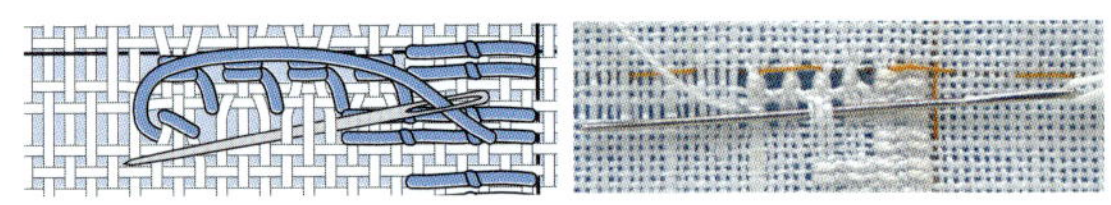

With the thread above the needle, take the needle under the first chysnytsia in the current row. Tighten the stitch so that it lies flat on the surface of the fabric. This creates the laid part of the Roman stitch.

*The thread should emerge from below the laid thread.*

9

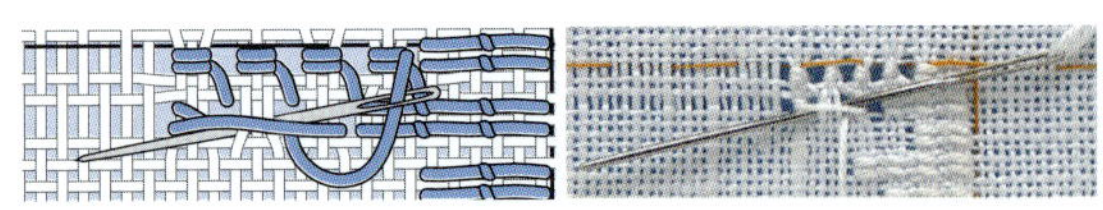

Take the needle diagonally under the second chysnytsia, entering from above the laid thread, and coming out below it.

*This is the first couching stitch over the laid thread.*

10

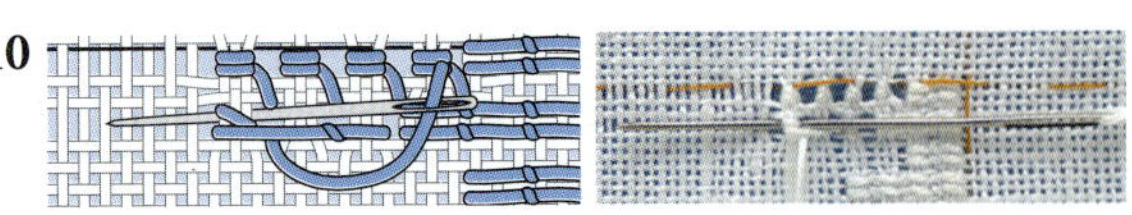

Above the laid thread, take the needle under the third chysnytsia, thus completing the first Roman stitch.

11 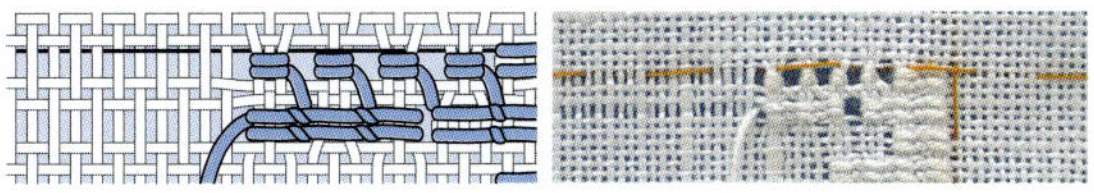

Work another Roman stitch above the first.

12 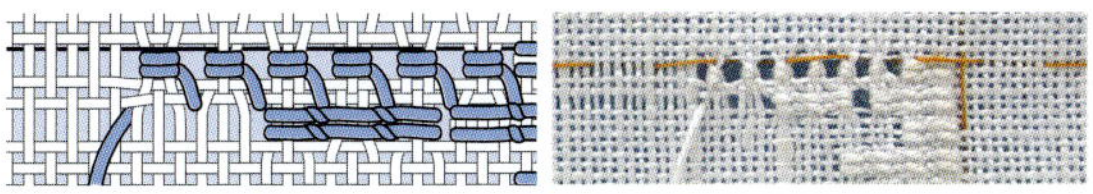

Work double wrap prutyk for the next two chysnytsi in Row 1.

13 

Work a layering of two Roman stitches over the next two chysnytsi in Row 2.

14 

Work the next double wrap prutyk in Row 1.

*In Row 2 there is a corresponding prutyk post, however it is not worked at this point. Instead it is worked with a double wrap prutyk as part of Row 3.*

15 

Continue following the pattern, working the double wrap prutyks in Row 1 and the layerings in Row 2. Leave the prutyk posts of Row 2 to be worked as part of Row 3.

## Row 3: layerings with prutyk

**In this row, layerings are worked, and the prutyk posts from the previous row are also completed.**

1 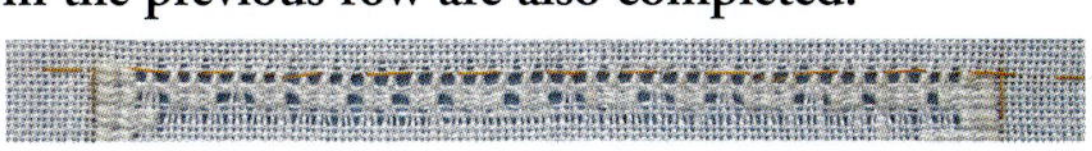

Moving down the drawn thread area, cut and remove the thread between the next Roman stitch pairs.

2 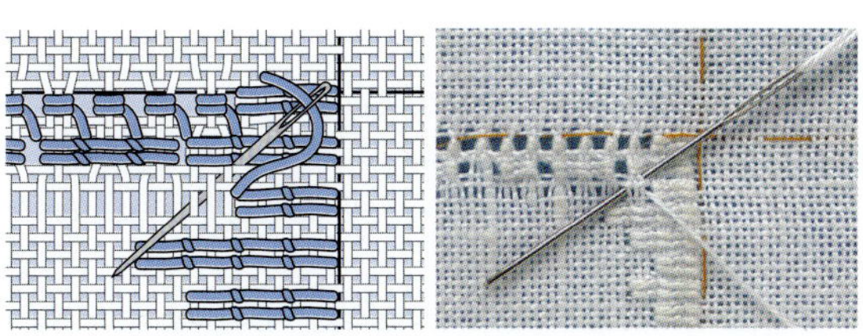

Bring the thread out in the space next to the Roman stitches at the end of Row 3. Diagonally take the needle under the woven section, from before the first chysnytsia in Row 2 to after the first chysnytsia in the current row. Gently tighten the stitch.

*This creates a small whip stitch over the woven section.*

3 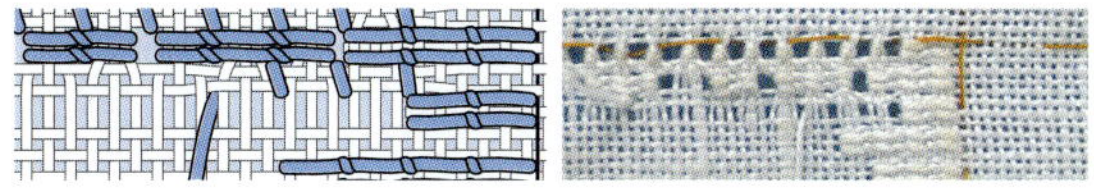

Whip the next two woven sections between chysnytsi.

4 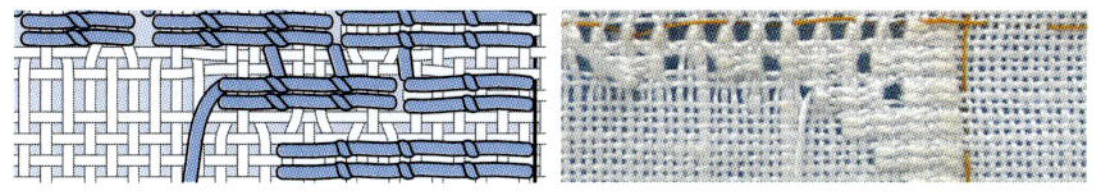

Work a layering in the current row over three chysnytsi.

5 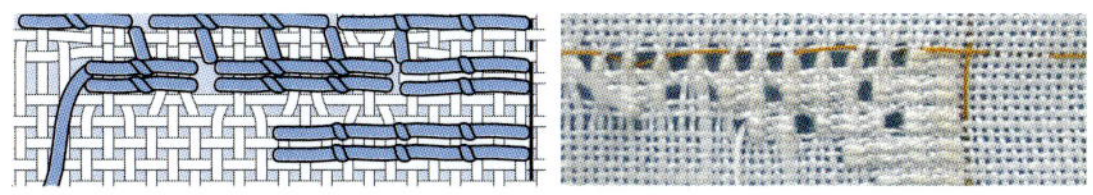

Whip the next two woven sections, then work a layering over two chysnytsi.

6 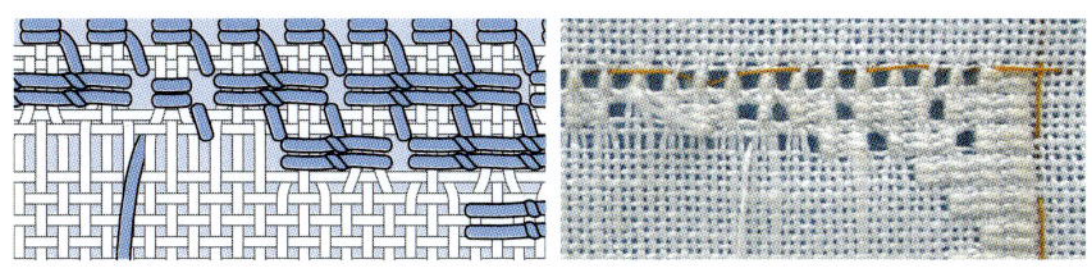

Whip the next two sections, then work a double wrap prutyk in Row 2.

*This leaves a space in the current row for a double wrap prutyk to be worked from the next row.*

7 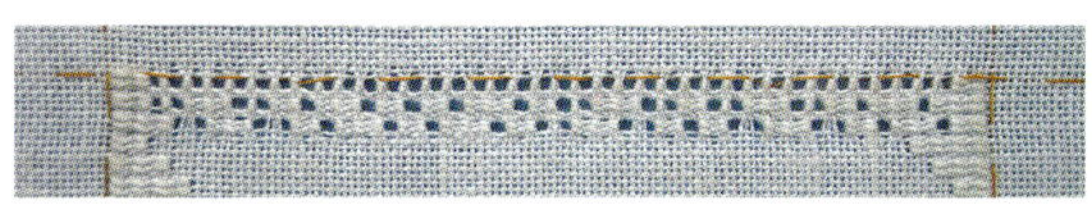

Continue following the pattern to the end of the row.

## Rows 4–8

1 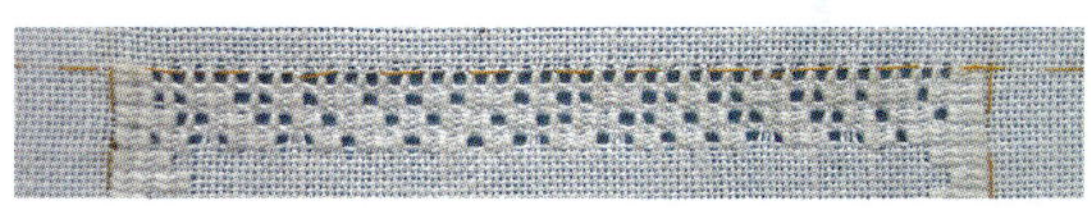

Work row 4 according to the chart.

2 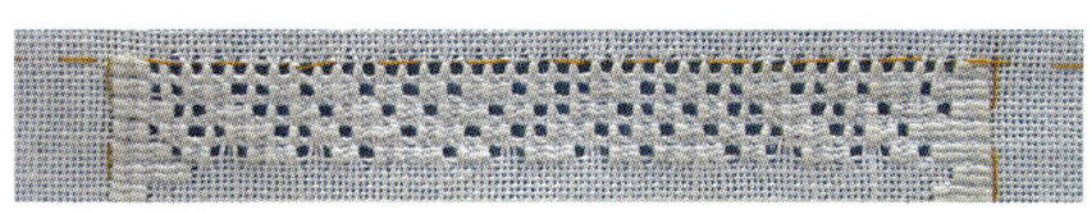

Work row 5 according to the chart.

3 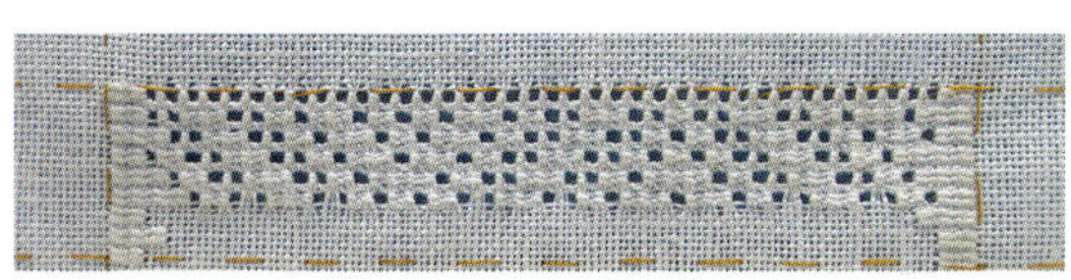

Work row 6 according to the chart.

4 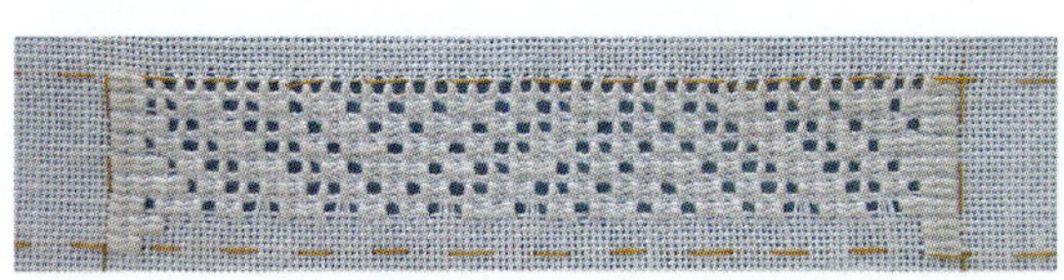

Work row 7 according to the chart.

5

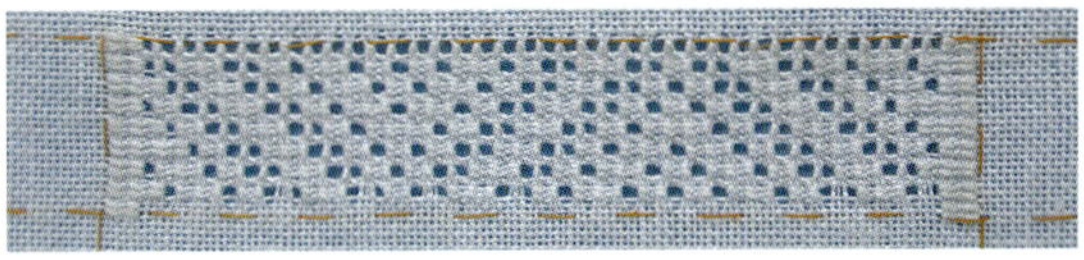

Work row 8 according to the chart.

## Row 9

**This is the final row and the only one where the double wrap prutyk posts are worked as part of the current row. Any prutyk posts remaining in the previous row are also worked.**

1

Bring the needle out next to the Roman stitch pair. Work a double wrap prutyk post in the previous row, bringing the needle out after the first chysnytsia in the current row. Gently tighten the stitch.

2

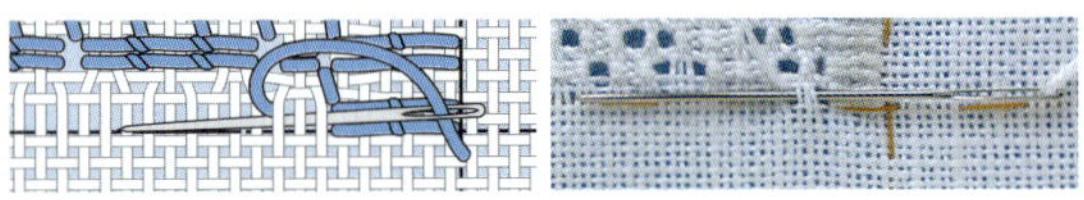

Take the needle under the first chysnytsia in the current row. Gently tighten the stitch.

3

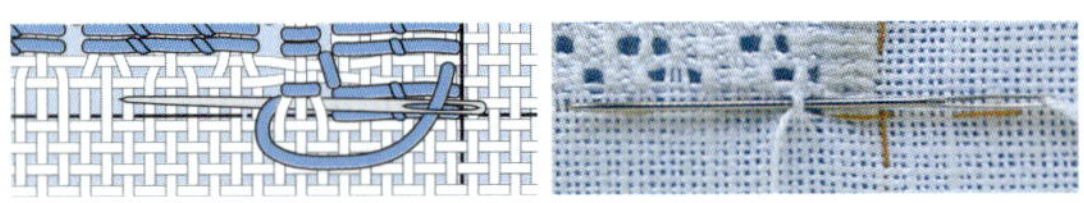

Take the needle under the first chysnytsia in the current row again and gently tighten the stitch, thus creating a double wrap prutyk.

4

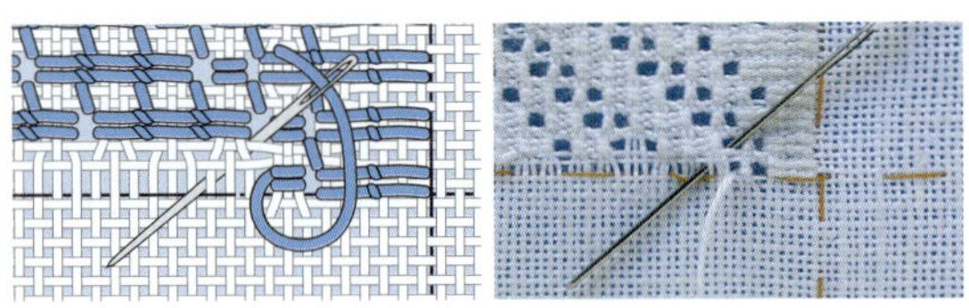

From before the second chysnytsia in the previous row, take the needle under the woven section to after the second chysnytsia in the current row.

5

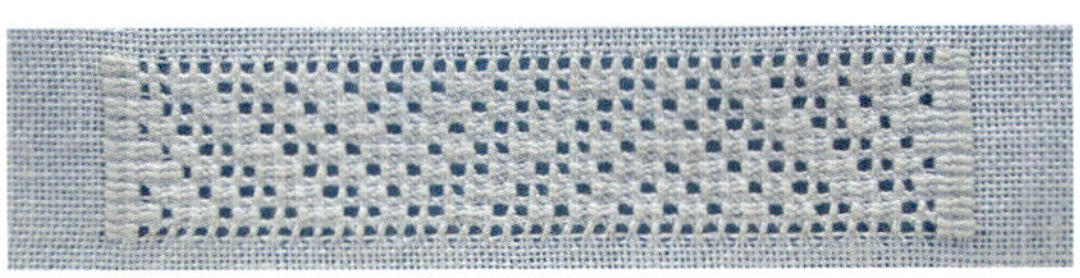

Continue following the pattern, completing any prutyk posts in the previous row, and working double wrap prutyk posts in the current row.

❶ *Remove the tacking.*

## Zig-zag border

**A simple zig-zag border of straight stitches is worked at the top and bottom of the band.**

1

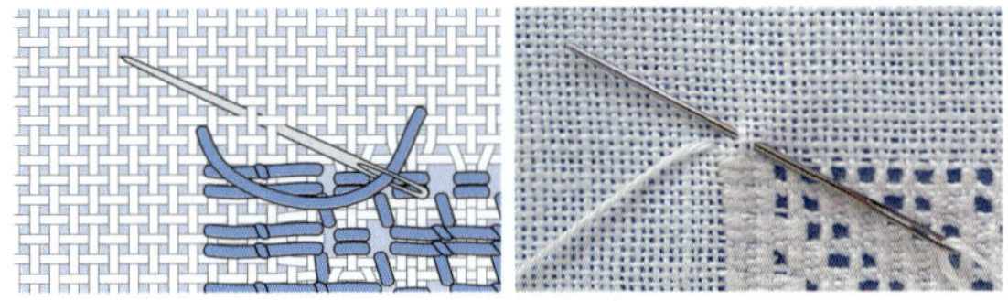

Work from left to right (vice versa for left-handers). Bring the needle out two threads above the top left Roman stitch. Insert the needle four threads to the right, and bring it out again two threads left and one thread up.

2

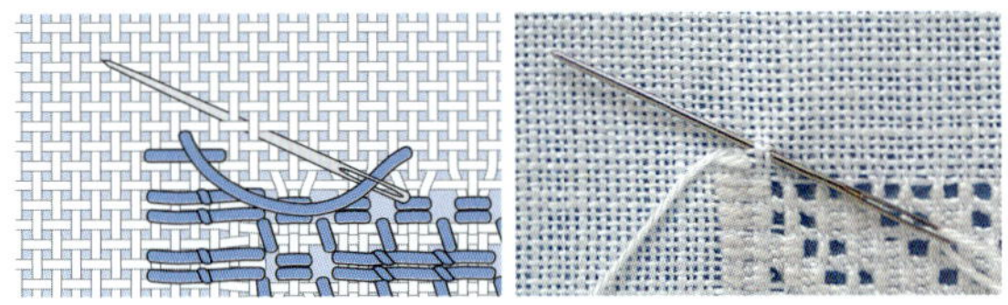

Insert the needle four threads to the right, and bring it out again two threads left and one thread up.

3

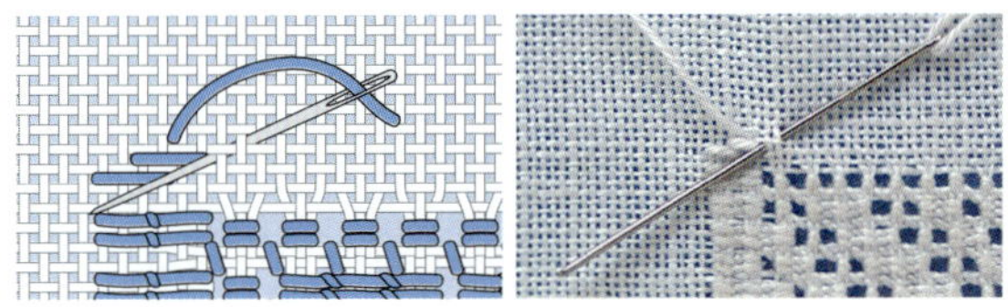

Insert the needle four threads to the right, and bring it out again two threads left and one thread down.

4

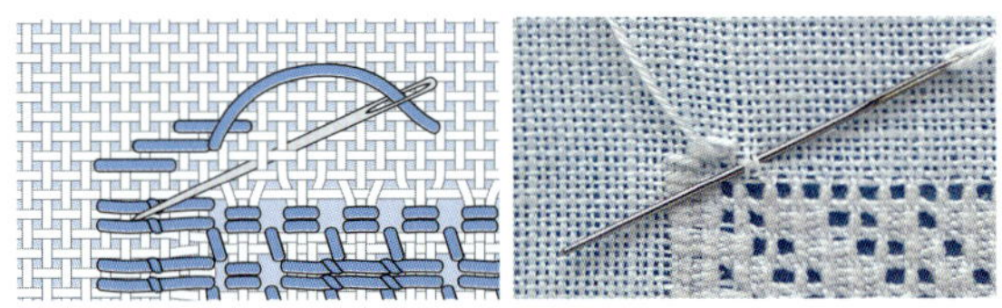

Insert the needle four threads to the right, and bring it out again two threads left and one down.

5

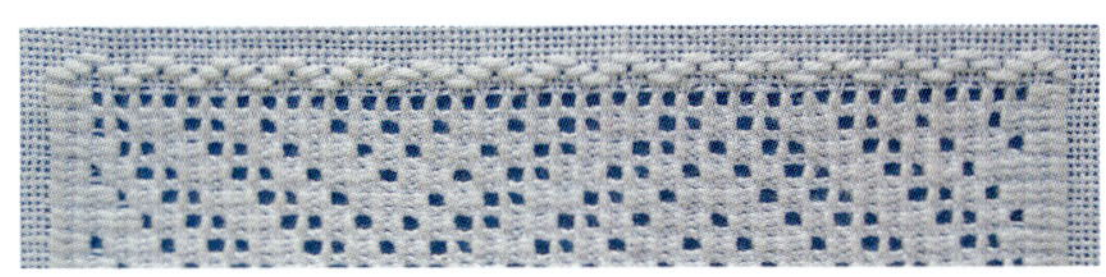

Continue zig-zagging in this pattern, across to the far side of the band.

❶ *Note that the last stitch only spans three threads, not four.*

6

Repeat the zig-zag border, mirrored according to the pattern, at the bottom of the band.

CHAPTER 4

# Additional techniques

## Starting and finishing a thread

**To make a seamless thread transition while stitching merezhka, cease stitching with the old thread between two layerings or prutyk, not during them.**

1 
To finish the thread, take it under seven unworked chysnytsi. Bring it out between the two woven threads.

2 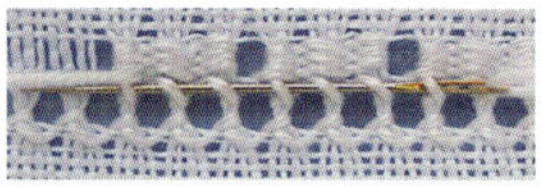
Start the new thread by running it under about seven stitches on the back.

3 Turn the fabric over. Resume working, catching the old thread into the back of the stitching. Upon reaching the thread end, carefully cut off any excess.

## Corners

**Merezhka Poltavska was traditionally worked in long straight bands, with no corners. Contemporary stitchers have wanted to use merezhka in rectangular and square designs, inventing non-traditional corner treatments. Many variations are possible.**

### SATIN STITCH MOTIF

**The bars are ended with satin or Roman stitch. A square satin stitch motif of choice is placed in the corner as decoration.**

### MITRED LAYERINGS

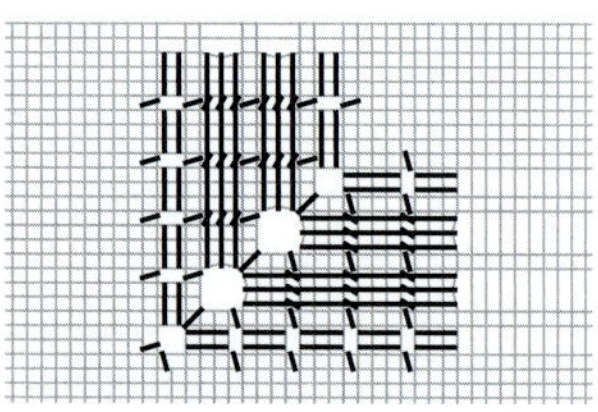

**This corner technique continues the layerings until they meet in the corner, forming a mitre. The example has four threads per chysnytsia.**

1 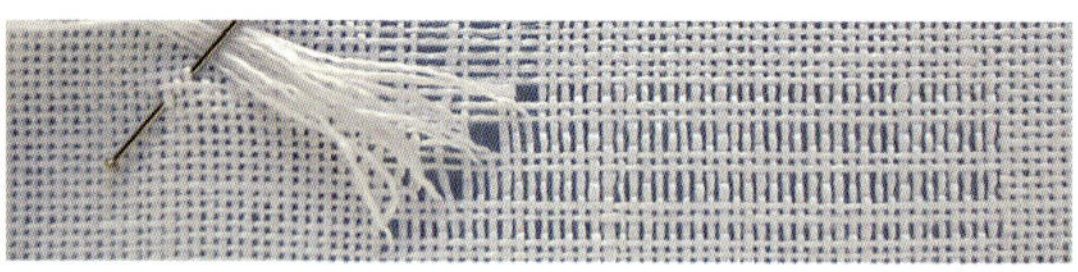

Cut and draw back the threads indicated on the chart. Fasten the threads out of the way with a pin.

2 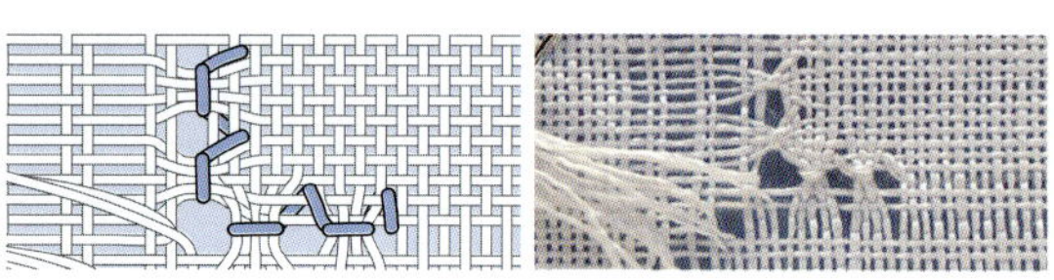

Hemstitch the inside edge.

❶ *Each corner bundle has five threads. All others have four.*

3 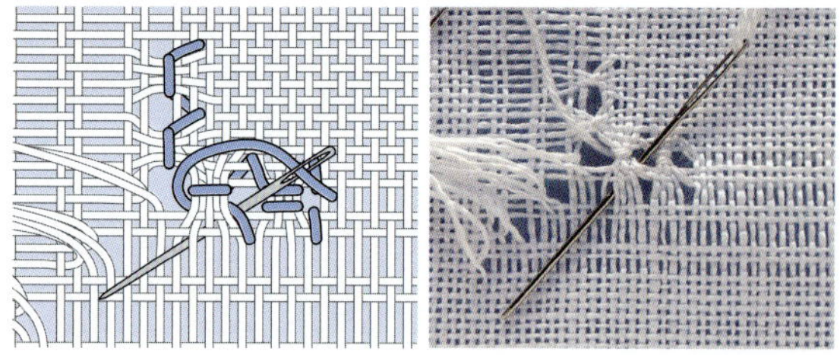

To start the next row, work prutyk in the previous row in preparation for the layerings. Though the bundle at the corner has five threads in the previous row, take the needle only under the usual four in this row.

4 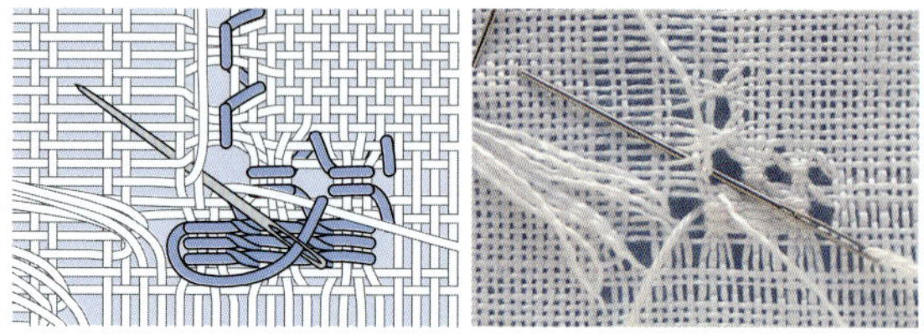

Work a layering. Release the current row's fastened fabric threads. Fold them out of the way. Take the needle under the first woven section on the next side, to create a whip stitch in the corner.

5 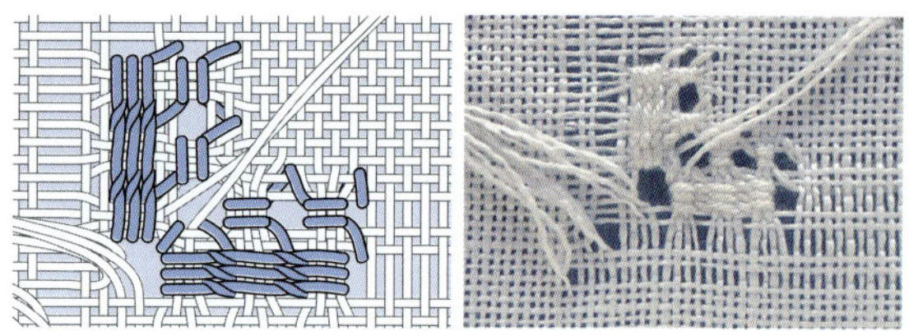

Pin the loose fabric threads towards the inside corner. Complete the prutyk and layering on the next side.

6 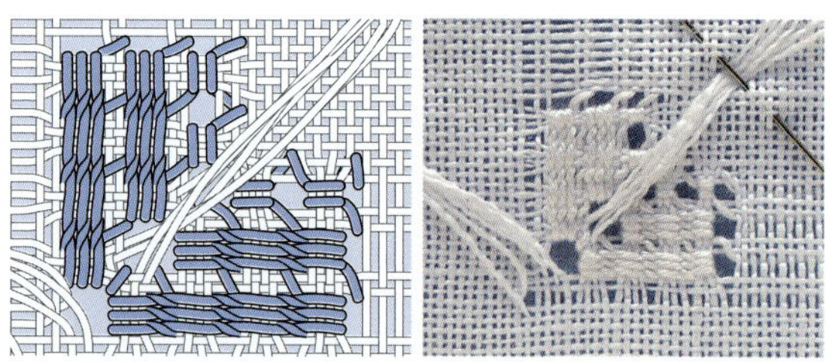

Work the layerings in the next row, turning the corner similarly to the previous row.

7 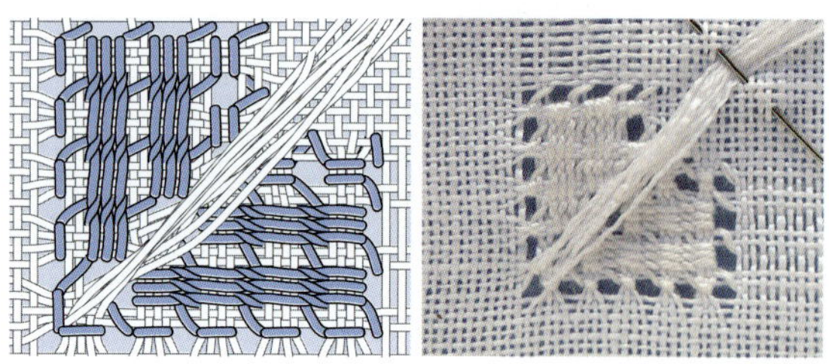

Release the fastened threads and work prutyk for the next row. Make sure there are once again five threads in each of the corner bundles. Pin the unfastened threads towards the inside corner.

8

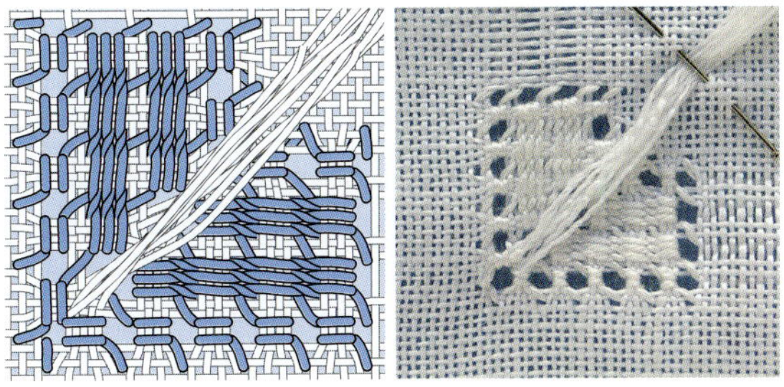

Work prutyk on the outside edge of the corner, with five threads in each corner bundle.

9

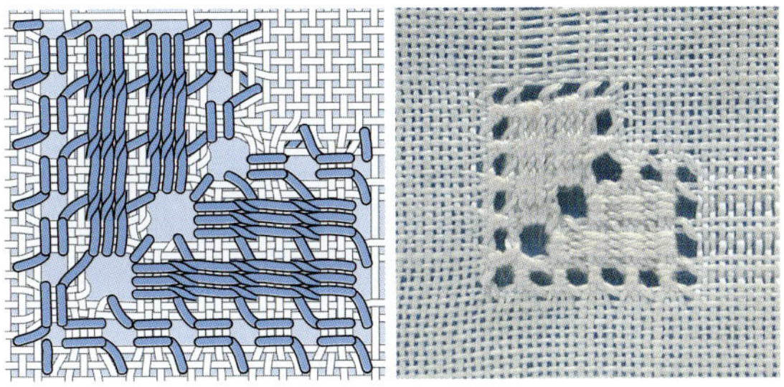

Take the threads through to the back. Neatly run them under the stitching, parallel to the layerings, for the distance of about five chysnytsi. Trim any excess.

## WRAPPED BULLION

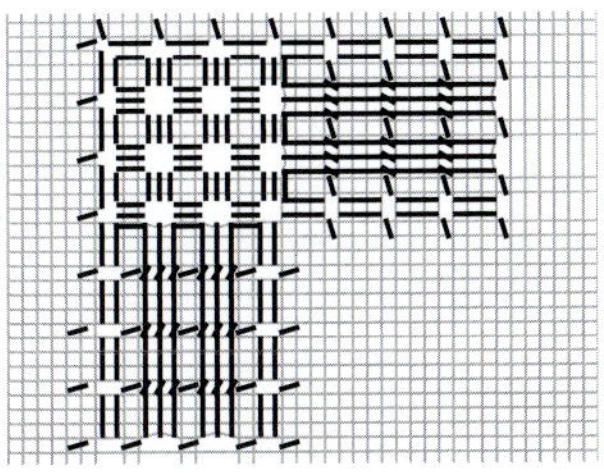

**Wrapped bars that look like bullion knots are created at the intersection of the bands for this corner variation. It is a firm and sturdy form of corner treatment.**

1

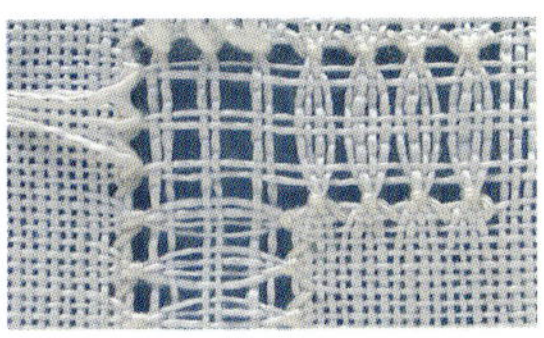

Hemstitch the inside and outside edges of the corner. Cut and draw back the threads for each row as shown.

2 Take the loose fabric thread ends to the back, and fasten them out of the way.

3

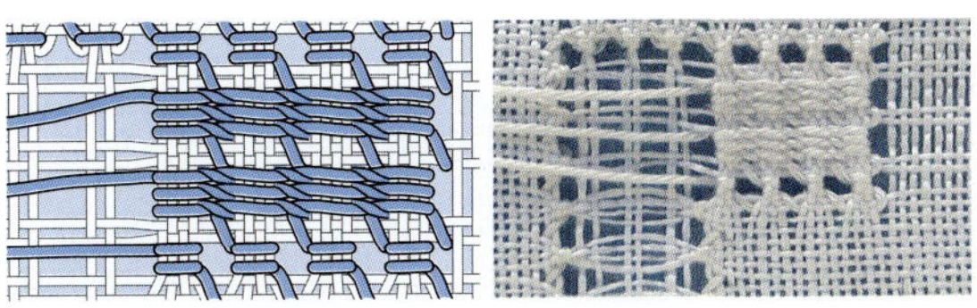

Work the layerings and prutyk for the first side.

4

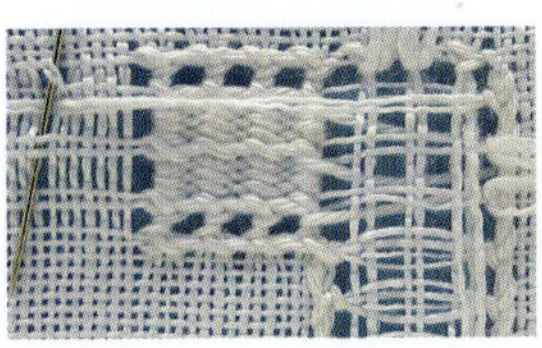

Turn the work over. Unfasten the thread ends closest to the outside edge. Pin them along the rows.

5

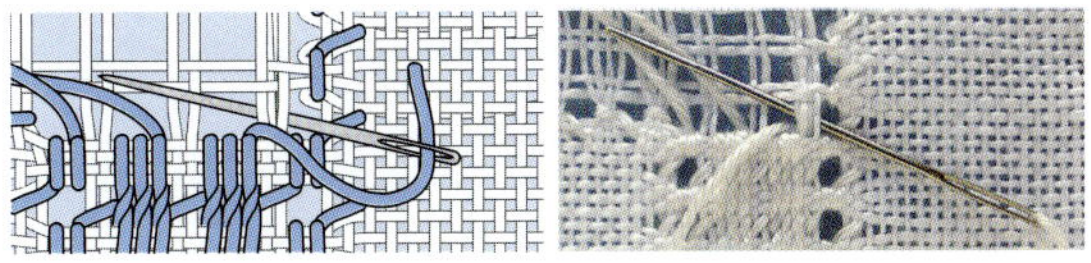

Turn the work back over to the front. Catching in the threads on the back, take the needle under the bar adjacent to the layering. Gently tighten the stitch.

6

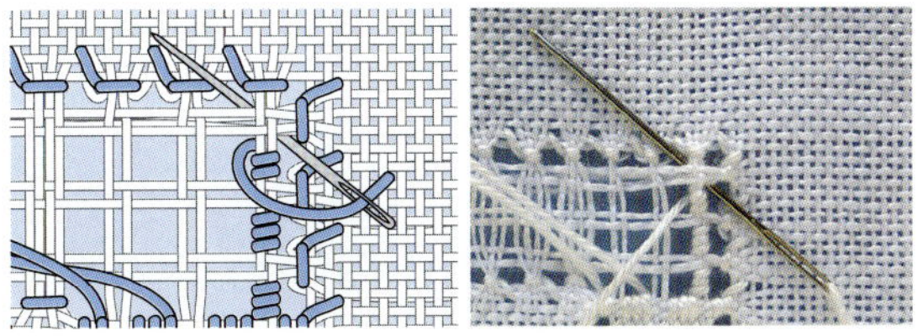

Wrap the bars three times each. To work the last stitch, take the needle diagonally under the last cross bar.

❶ *Ensure the threads on the back are caught into the stitching.*

7

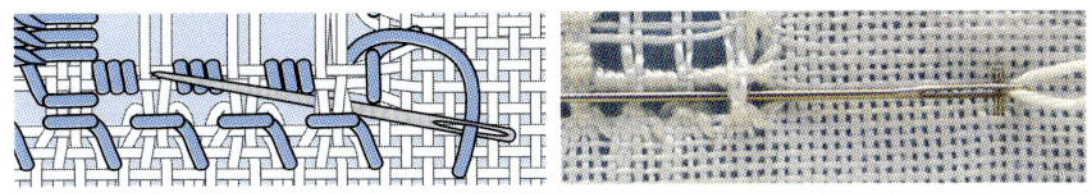

Turn the work 90 degrees clockwise. Take the needle under the first bar of the new side from right to left.

❶ *This wraps the end bar of the previous side, once.*

8

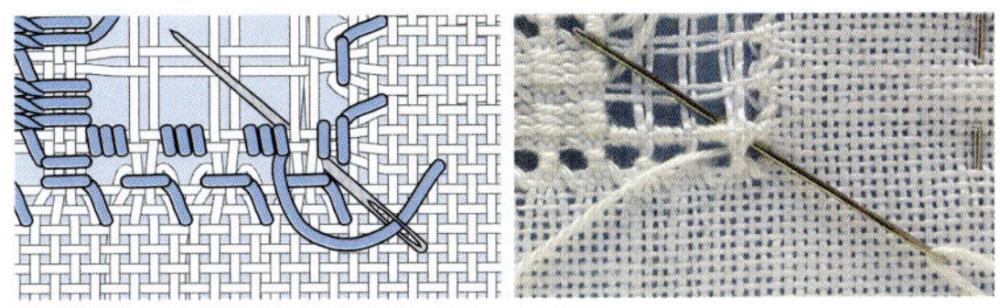

Take the needle diagonally under the cross bar.

❶ *This wraps the end bar of the current side once, and positions the needle and thread ready to wrap the next bar.*

9

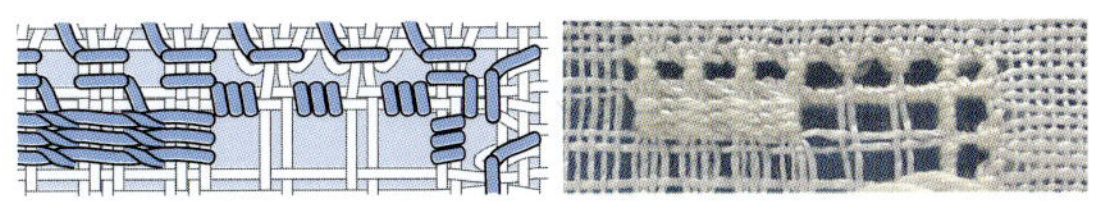

Turn the work 90 degrees anticlockwise. Wrap the bars three times each. Continue with prutyk and layerings.

10 Turn the work over. Trim the excess fabric thread ends from the completed row. Lay the thread ends for the next row along and pin them in place.

11

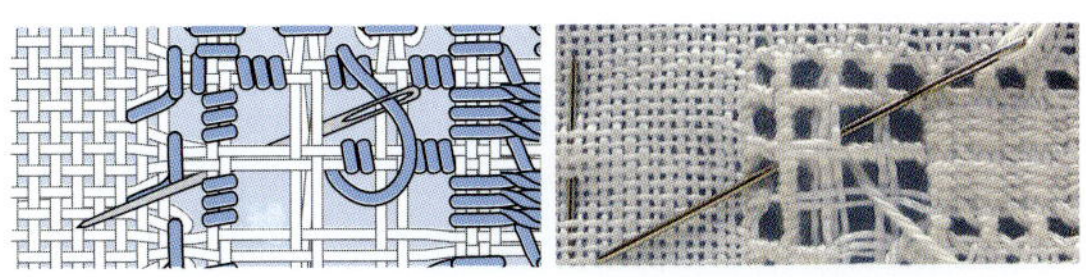

Turn over to the front, and wrap the first two bars, catching in all the threads laid along the back. Take the needle diagonally under the next two cross bars.

❶ *This positions the needle ready to work back towards the already complete wrapped bars.*

12 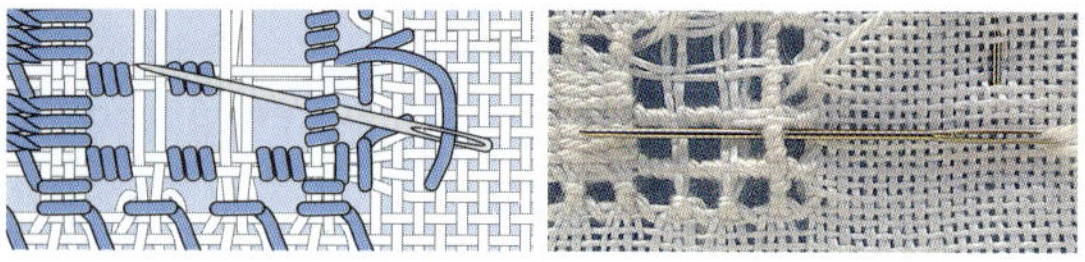

Turn the work 180 degrees, and take the needle under the bar as shown.

13 Wrap the bar between those already complete, covering all threads laid along the back of the bar.

14 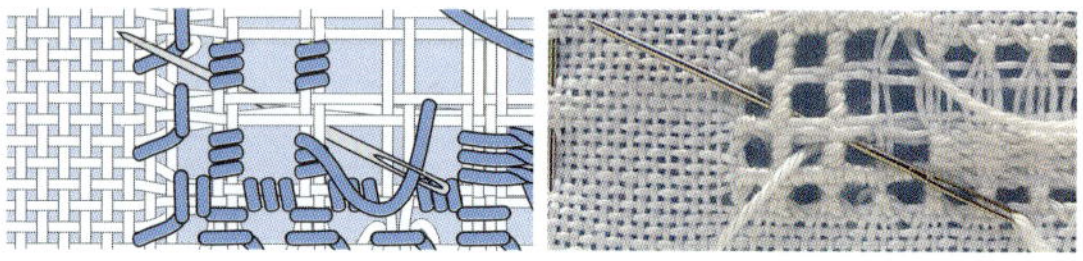

Turn the work 180 degrees again. Take the needle under the two cross bars.

15 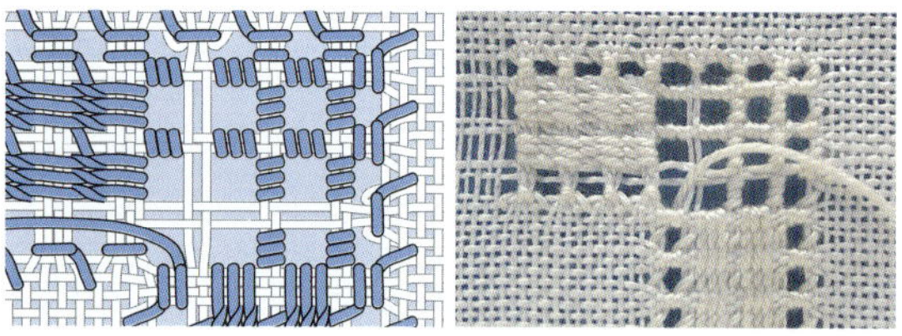

Turn the work 180 degrees. Work the entire row, beginning with one stitch over the first bar, then three wraps for each bar. Continue the row with the layerings.

❶ *Ensure all threads laid along the back are caught in.*

16 

Work the remaining row by wrapping up to the first cross bar. Lace the thread to the far end of the row, then work back, covering all the laid threads. From the cross bar, lace the thread to the beginning of the new side. Work the row, catching in the laid threads.

# Hems

## PRUTYK

**Prutyk is also a hemming technique. The sample uses a hem which is 10 mm (3/8 in) wide.**

1 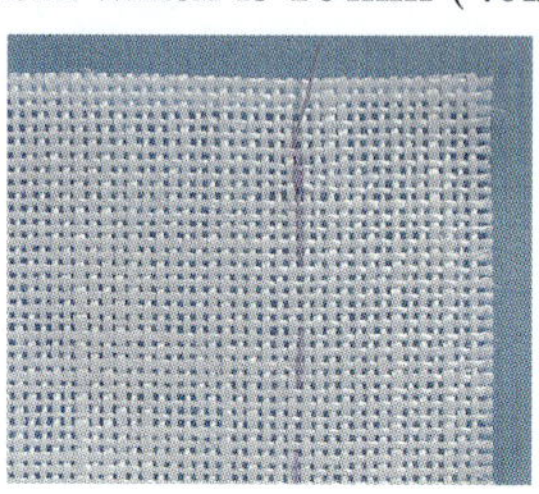

Near the right end of the hem, run a line of tacking from the edge of the fabric, for a distance of about 40 mm (1 1/2 in).

2 

Measure 30 mm (1 3/16 in) in from the top edge of the fabric. Remove a thread across the fabric at this point.

3 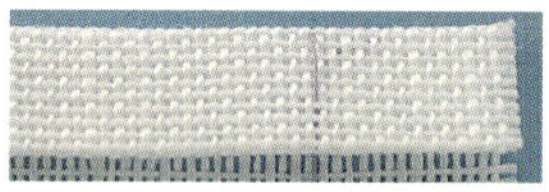

Fold in 10 mm (3/8 in) twice, to meet the missing thread, to create the hem.

❶ *Match the tacking lines to each other to ensure that all the fabric threads align properly through the folds.*

4 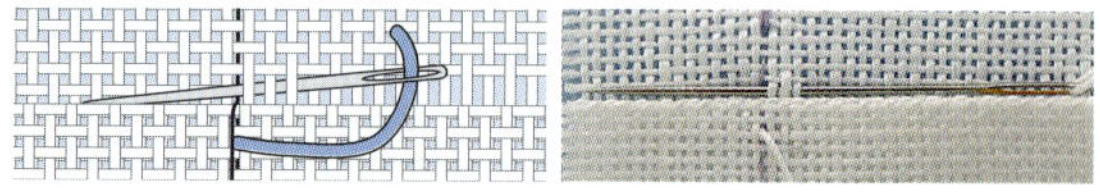

Turn the work 180 degrees, so that the hem is at the bottom. At the left end of the hem, bring the needle out two threads down from the hem fold. Take the needle from right to left, under the first group of three threads where the fabric thread was removed.

❶ *The stitching is worked from left to right (and vice versa for left-handers), and on the back of the fabric.*

5 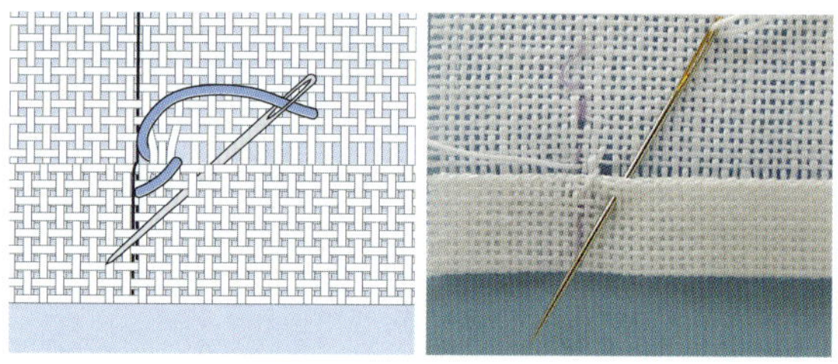

Insert the needle in the back of the hem fold. Bring it out three threads along from where it first emerged.

❶ *The needle does not go through the front fabric at this point, only the hem fold.*

❶ *By moving along in groups of threes each time at both the front and the back of the fabric, the fabric will not pucker.*

6 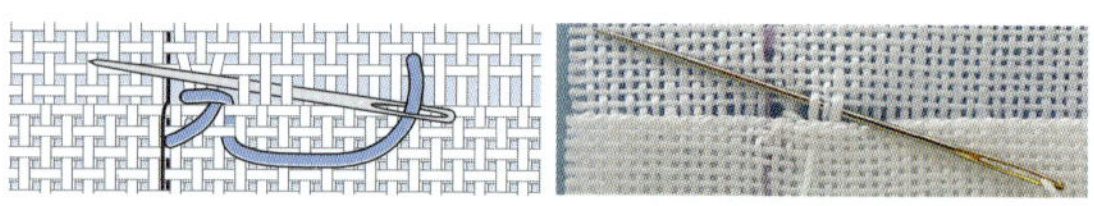

Take the needle under the next group of three threads.

7 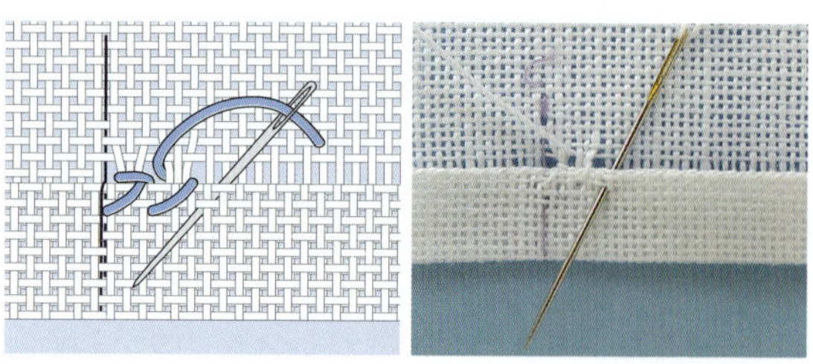

Insert the needle in the back of the hem fold, bringing it out three threads along from the previous stitch.

8 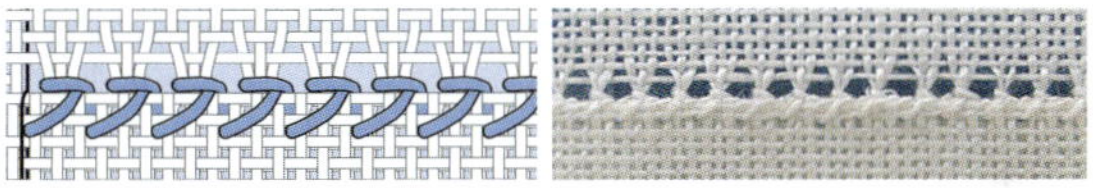

Continue in the same manner to complete the hem.

! 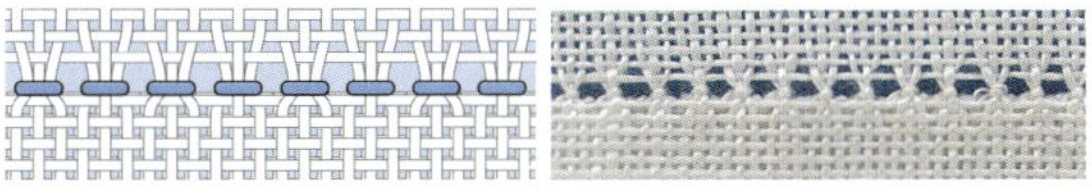

*The front shows only short stitches across each chysnytsia.*

## BACK STITCH

**This simple hem has parallel lines of back stitch to hold the hem in place. The sample uses a hem which is 10 mm (3/8 in) wide.**

1 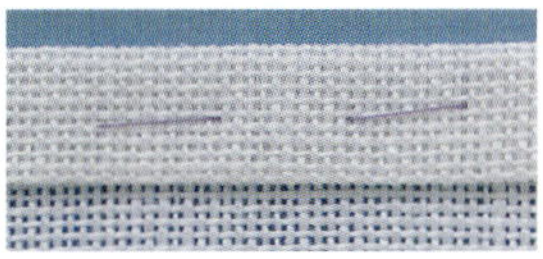

Fold in 10 mm (3/8 in) twice to create the hem. Baste it in place.

2 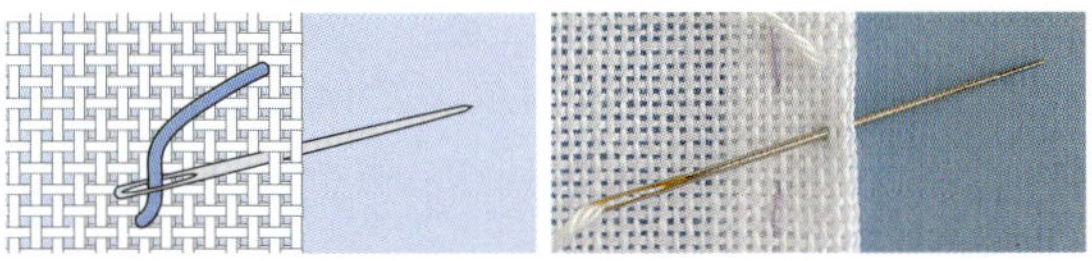

Turn the work over and then 90 degrees clockwise. Bring the needle out four threads along from the beginning of the line of stitching, and two threads away from the fold. Insert the needle at the beginning of the line.

! *Insert the needle directly from the front to the back so that the fabric threads remain aligned.*

3 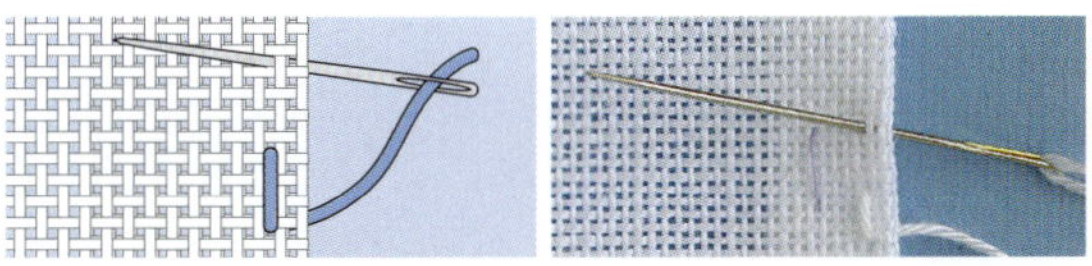

Bring the needle out four threads past the previous stitch.

4 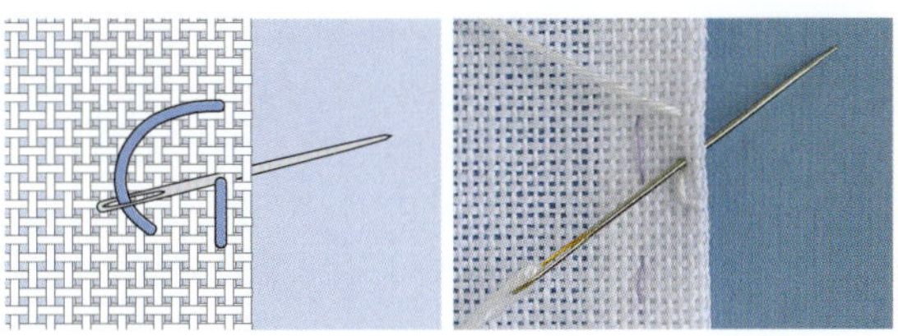

Insert the needle through the same hole as the end of the previous stitch.

! *Each stitch is worked from its far end, back to meet the previous stitch.*

5 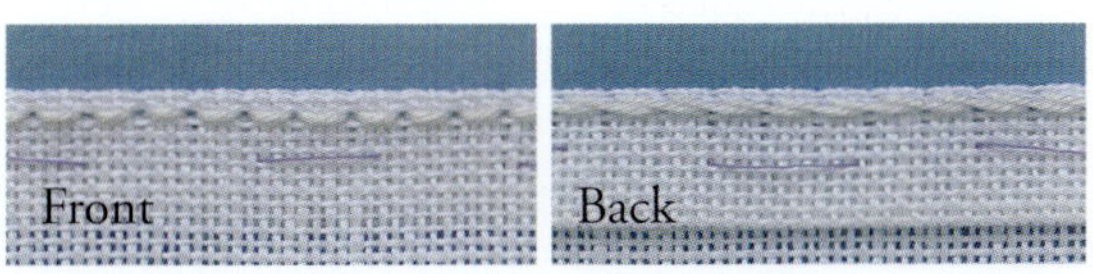


Complete the line of back stitch. The back should be as neat as possible as it will be visible.

6 

Work additional lines of back stitching, aligning with the first. The example shows the first line, a space of two threads, another line, a space of four threads, then another line of back stitch.

! *With a wider hem, more lines and other spacing variations could be used.*

## TOOTH EDGE

**This tooth edge can be combined with hem finishes. Traditionally it featured on collars, cuffs and shirt hems.**

1 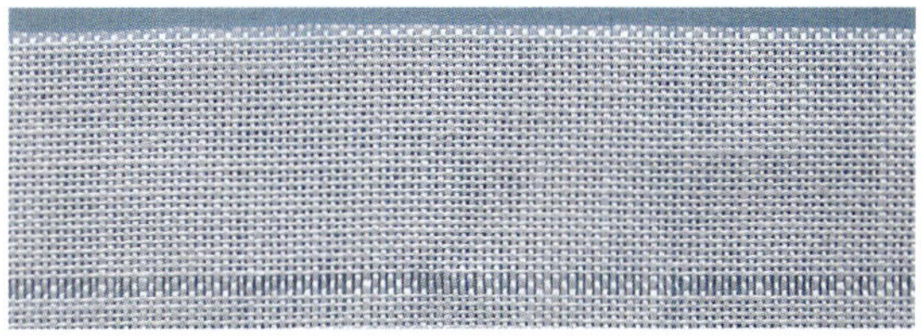

Remove two threads for the fold at the hem edge.

2 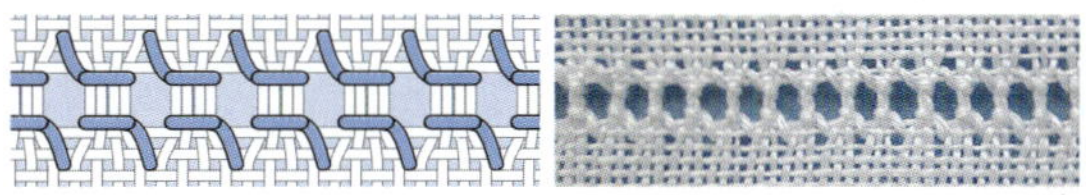

Work double prutyk (hemstitch) down each side of the withdrawn threads.

3 

Fold the hem to the back, with the fold along the centre of the double prutyk.

4 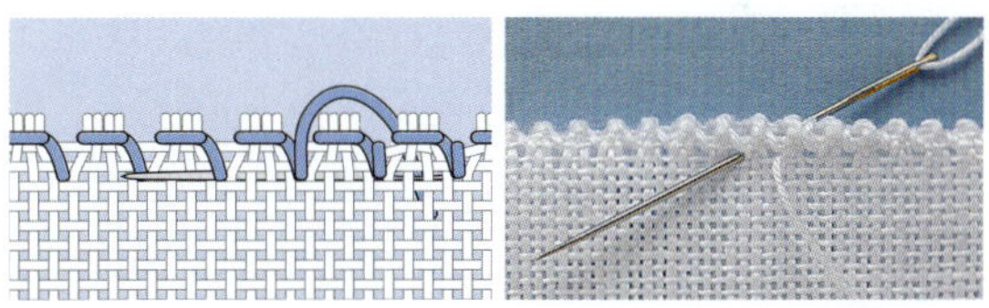

To overcast between the teeth, bring the needle out through the prutyk stitching holes on the front. Gently tighten each stitch to make the teeth more pronounced.

5 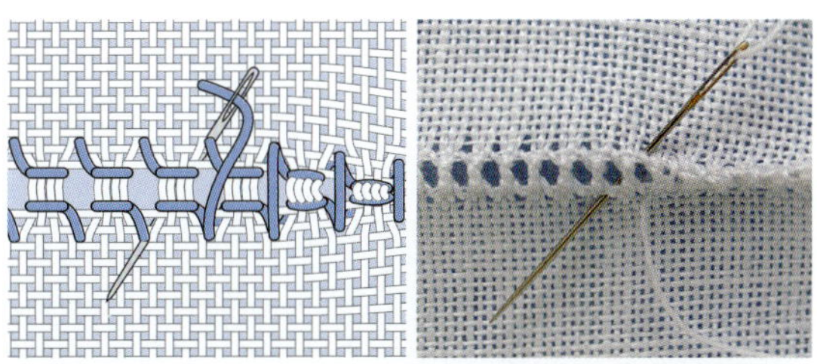

Insert the needle in the aligning hole at the back. To neatly move along, take the needle inside the fabric fold, bringing it out between the next two teeth. Gently tighten each stitch to emphasise the teeth.

6

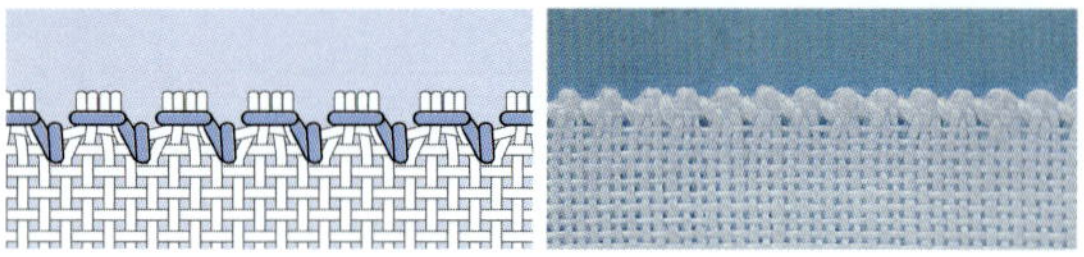

The finished hem fold. Hem as desired.

### MITRED CORNERS

1

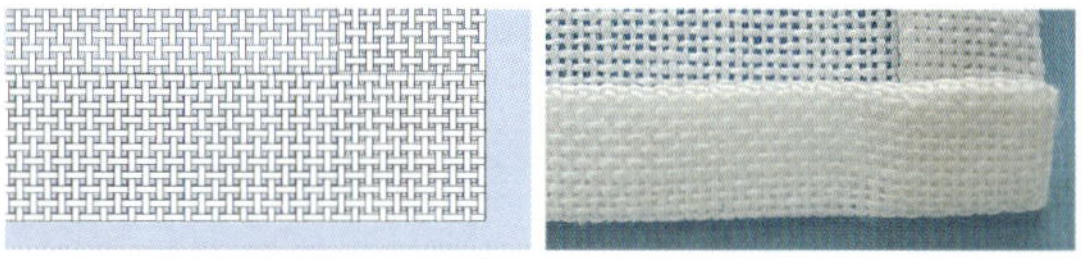

Fold in one third of the hem allowance, and then another third. Press the folds in place.

2

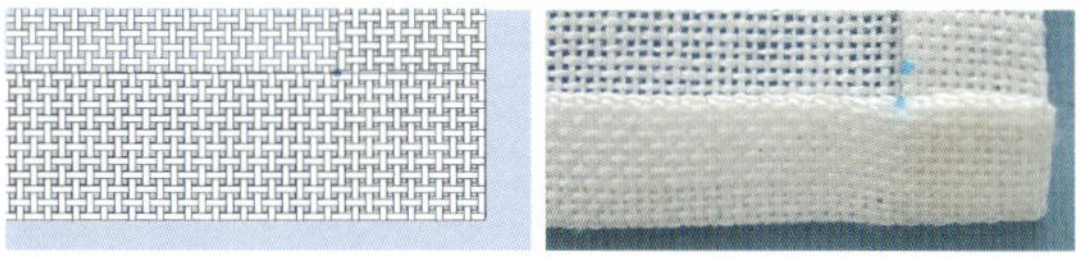

Using a blue dressmaker's pencil, lightly mark the intersection of inner edges of the hems, as shown.

3

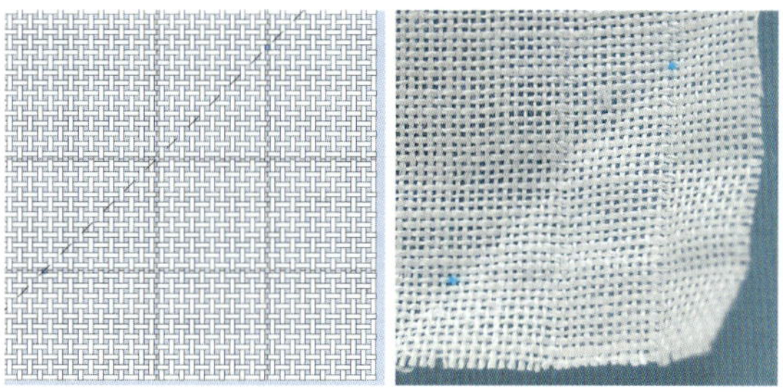

Unfold the hems. Diagonally make a fold through the two marked points, across the corner. Unfold

! *The crease is the stitching line for the mitre.*

4

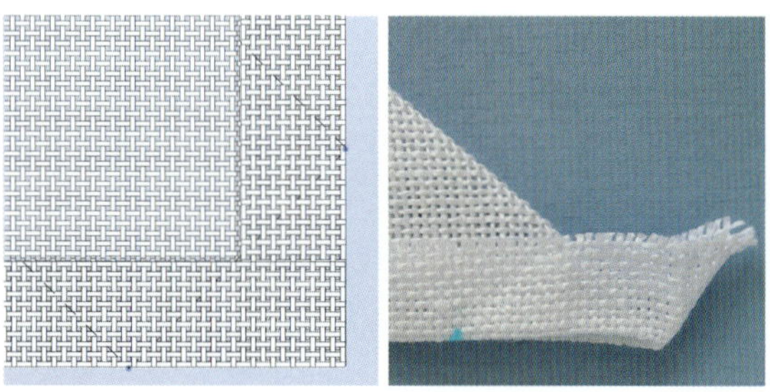

Refold the first hem folds (above left), and with right sides together, fold the fabric diagonally (above right), through the corner.

5

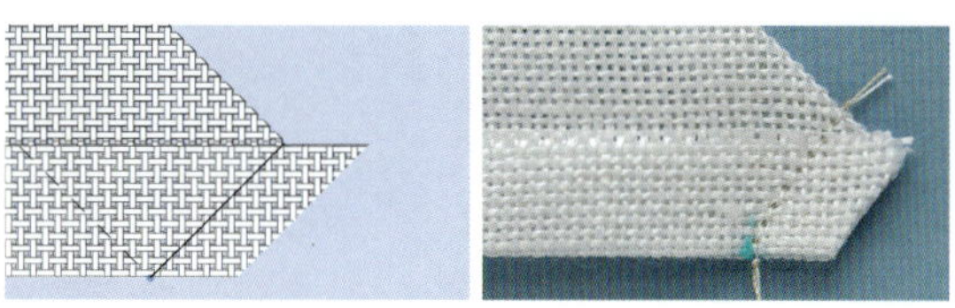

Sew along the mitre stitching line, keeping the first hem fold in place. Trim the mitre seam allowance to 6 mm (1/4 in).

6

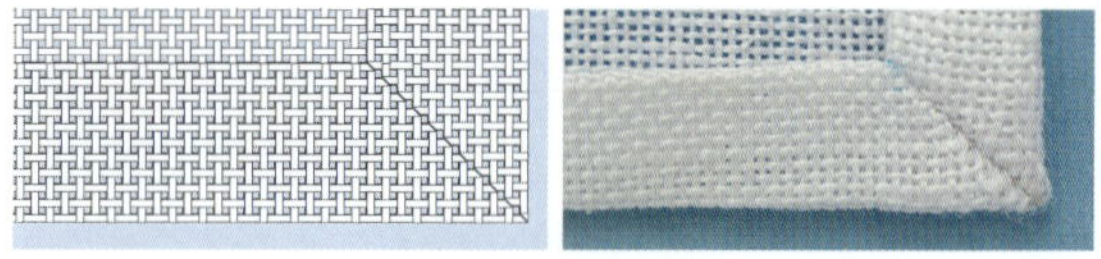

Turn the corner the right way out, with the seam open flat and the first hem fold tucked inside hem.

## Cross stitch

**Cross stitch is often worked in conjunction with merezhka. The individual cross method shown here accentuates the colour gradations when using overdyed thread. All crosses should have their top stitch lying in the same direction. Each cross stitch is worked over a square of two by two fabric threads.**

1

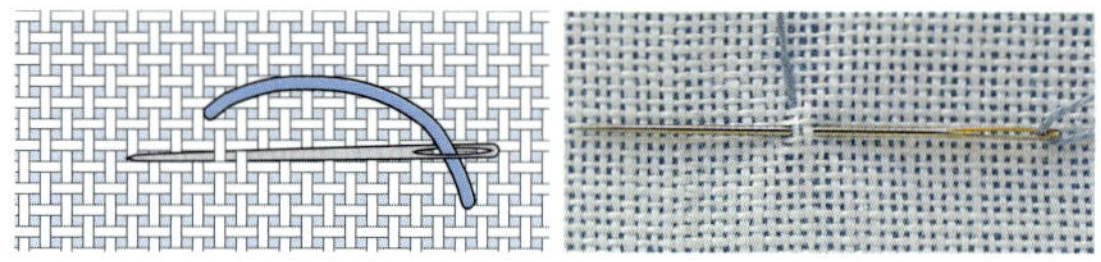

Bring the needle out in the top left corner of a two by two thread square. Insert the needle in the bottom right corner, and bring it out again in the bottom left corner.

2

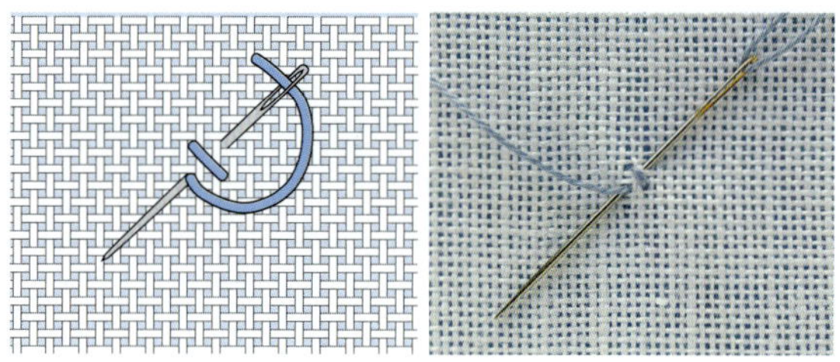

Insert the needle from the top right to the bottom left, to complete the first cross.

3

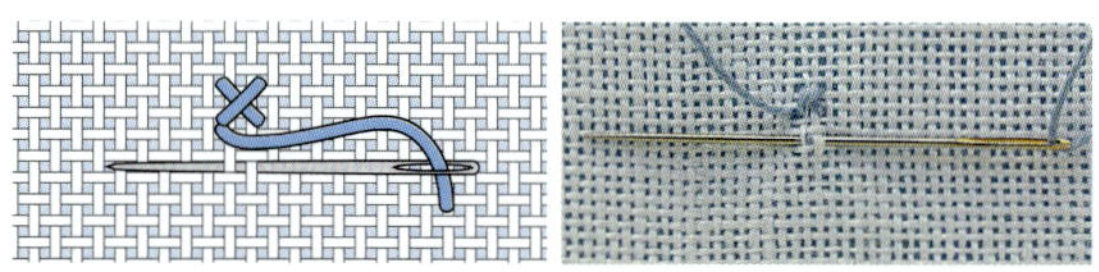

Insert the needle in the bottom right corner, and bring it out again in the bottom left corner.

4

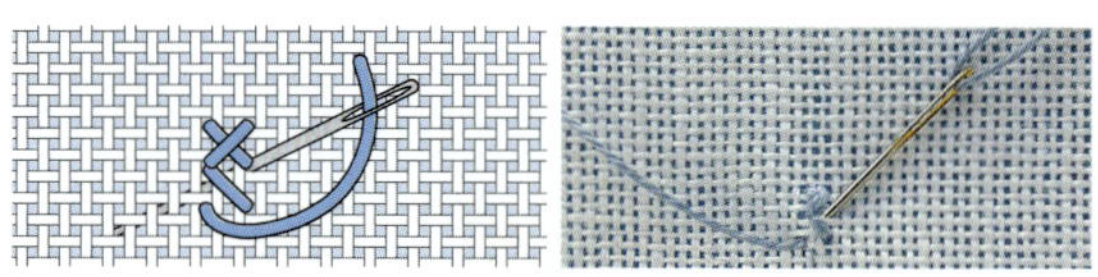

Insert the needle in the top right corner, thus completing the second cross stitch.

5

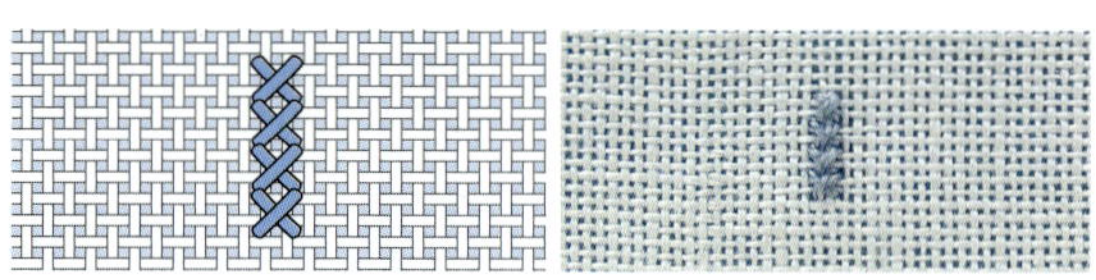

Continue stitching in the same way to build up the pattern as required.

CHAPTER 5

# Merezhka Poltavska projects

# Bookmark

**With no prutyk except for the edge rows, this bookmark is a great introductory project. It features tooth-edged hems along the sides which are unusual because they fold to the front rather than the back.**

FINISHED SIZE 5 x 23cm (2 x 9in)
TECHNIQUE Large scale Merezhka Poltavska
MATERIALS NEEDED

- 15 x 25cm (6 x 10in), 28 count linen, white
- 23m (25yd) Medium thread, white (see 'Compatibility', p7)
- No 24 tapestry needle

EMBROIDERY

❶ *Careful counting will assist with the correct positioning of the embroidery and its motifs.*

1 Fold the short side of the fabric in half. Along the fold, measure 5cm (2in) in from one end of the fabric. Run a line of tacking perpendicular to the fold.
2 Count 16 threads from the fold, along the tacked line.
3 Working across four threads, stitch a bar of satin stitch with 31 stitches, just inside the tacked line.
4 Work counted tacking from both ends of the satin stitch down the length of the fabric, over and under groups of four threads.
5 Using the tacking, count 41 groups of four threads (164 threads). Run a line of tacking across the fabric.
6 Inside the tacking, work another bar of 31 satin stitches.
7 Cut and remove the top two threads between the two satin stitch bars.
8 Work hemstitch along the outer edge of the removed threads, grouping the threads into fours.
9 Moving downwards, skip two threads. Cut and withdraw the next two threads between the satin stitch bars.

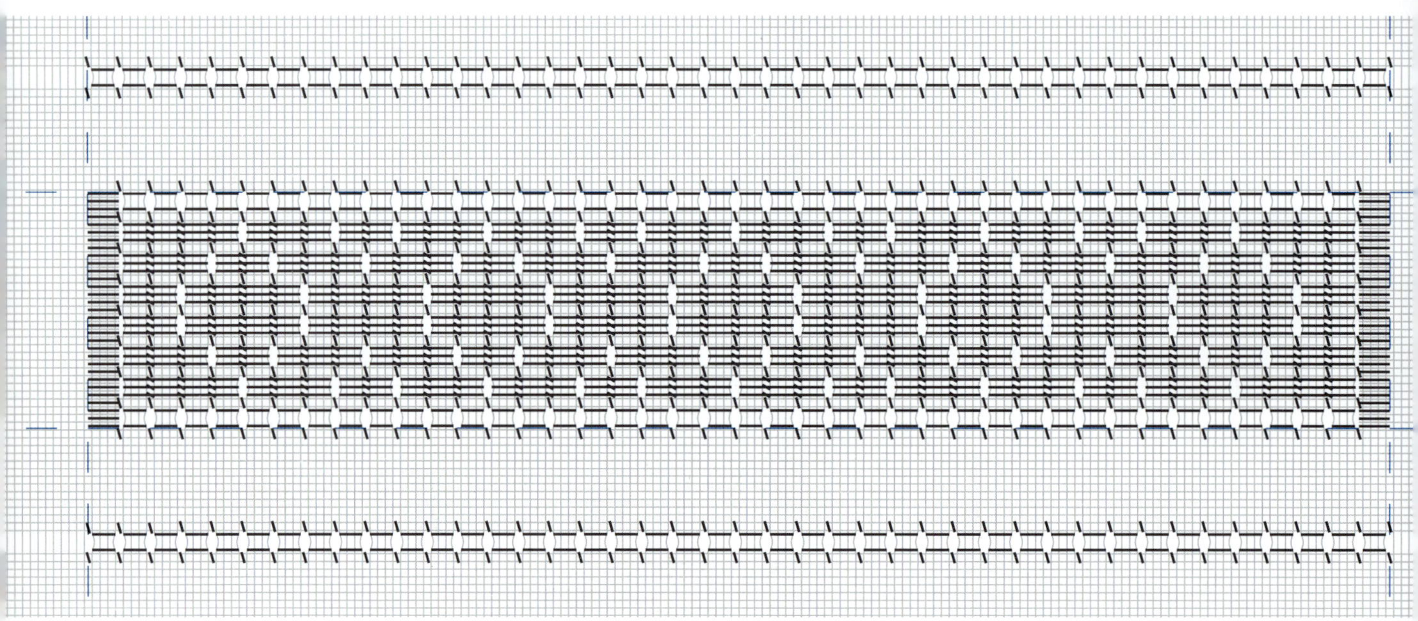

**10** Following the chart, complete the first row's prutyk posts and work the layerings in the current row.

**11** Work the remainder of the merezhka rows, finishing with prutyk on the opposite side of the band.

## TOOTH-EDGED HEM

**1** Count 14 threads out from the outermost removed thread and remove the 15th and 16th threads.

**2** Turn the fabric over. Starting and finishing at the tacked guides, work double prutyk down each side of the withdrawn threads.

❶ *The hemstitching is worked on the back of the fabric because the hems will be folded to the front.*

❶ *The tooth edge technique is described in detail on page 29.*

**3** Fold the hem to the front, with the fold along the centre of the double prutyk, thereby creating teeth. Overcast between each of the teeth.

**4** Trim the hem allowance to ten threads. Fold the hem allowance in half, tucking the raw edge inside the hem.

**5** Through the same holes as the base of the prutyk, work back stitch.

❶ *Make sure the back-stitching is as neat as possible on the reverse of the bookmark, as it will be visible.*

**6** Count four threads in and work a corresponding line of back stitch.

**7** Remove all basting.

## FRINGED ENDS

**1** Count 50 threads out from each satin stitch bar, and trim the fabric at this point.

**2** Remove the threads at the end of the bookmark, all the way to the satin stitch.

❶ *Take care not to accidentally remove any of the threads which are cut on the inside edge of the satin stitch bar.*

# Bell pull

**On historical works featuring cross stitching in black, sometimes the thread looks like it has faded from black to grey. This is because during the dyeing process, linen does not absorb black dye well. This bell pull uses a black overdyed thread to approximate this effect.**

SIZE 13.5 x 46 cm (5 3/8 x 18 in)
TECHNIQUE Large scale Merezhka Poltavska
MATERIALS

- 70 x 20 cm (27 1/2 x 8 in) Dublin linen 25 count, cream
- 46 m (50 yd), Thick thread, ecru/natural (to match linen) (see 'Compatibility', p7)
- 2 skeins stranded floss, Weeks Dye Works #3900 Kohl (or other brand of black/grey overdyed stranded floss)
- 15 cm (6 in) bell pull hangers, black
- No 22 tapestry needle
- machine sewing thread to match linen

## EMBROIDERY

❶ *Careful counting will assist with the correct positioning of the embroidery and its motifs.*

1 Measure 8 cm (3 3/16 in) from one end of the fabric, and baste a line across the short width of the fabric.
2 Fold the fabric in half across the tacked line, to find the centre. Mark with a pin.
3 From the pin, count 29 threads across to one side. From this point work the satin stitch bar (59 stitches, four threads wide) across the fabric, inside the line.
4 From the ends of the satin stitch bar, baste over and under 126 groups of three threads along the length of the fabric.
5 At the end of the counted tacking, work a satin stitch bar to match the first one.

❶ *There are three merezhka sections: A, B and C.*

6 Work the merezhka band down the fabric. Work Part A at the top, then Part B seven times, finishing with Part C at the bottom.

❶ *There are three cross stitch sections: A, B and C.*

7 Work the cross stitching beside the merezhka, using three strands of the Weeks Dye Works thread. Begin with Part A at the top. Follow this with Part B, repeating as necessary, and finish with Part C at the bottom of the satin stitched bands.

❶ *Cross stitches are worked over blocks of two by two threads: two threads across and two down.*

❶ *Work each cross fully before moving on to the next one, so that the overdyed colour variations are more pronounced.*

## FINISHING

1 From the bottom of the stitching, measure 8 cm down, and trim the extra fabric.
2 From the sides of the cross stitch, count out 14 threads, then remove the next thread, along the entire length of the fabric. Count out 30 more threads (the side hem allowance), and trim the fabric.
3 Fold in one third of the hem allowance, and then again, so that the fold meets the removed thread's space.
4 Work a prutyk hem (see page 28) down the fabric.

❶ *Make sure the threads of each chysnytsia align with those of the merezhka band.*

5 Repeat on the other side.
6 At the top and bottom, fold 2 cm (3/4 in) in, then another 2 cm (3/4 in) to form pockets for the hangers. Machine stitch 2 mm (1/16 in) from the inside edge of the pocket hem, across the width of the bell pull.
7 Remove any basting.
8 Slip the hangers into their pockets.

❶ *If your hangers have two different size hanging loops, the larger one is for weighting the bottom.*

## Scissors case

**Made to suit 9 cm ($3\frac{1}{2}$in) scissors, this gorgeous little scissors case will protect your embroidery scissors, while looking great.**

SIZE 10.5 x 6 cm ($4\frac{3}{16}$ x $2\frac{3}{8}$in)
TECHNIQUE Small scale Merezhka Poltavska
MATERIALS

- 10 x 14 cm (4 x $5\frac{1}{2}$in) 32 count linen, cream
- 23 m (25 yd) Medium thread, ecru/natural (see 'Compatibility', p7)
- 1 skein each No 5 pearl cotton, DMC 369 (very light pistachio green), DMC 778 (very light antique mauve)
- 1 skein stranded cotton, DMC 369 (very light pistachio green)
- 20 x 20 cm (8 x 8 in) buckram, medium weight
- No 24 tapestry needle
- No 9 embroidery needle
- 25 x 25 cm (10 x 10 in) dupion silk, pale green
- 20 x 20 cm (8 x 8 in) double-sided fusible webbing
- 3 cm ($1\frac{3}{16}$in) teardrop crystal bead
- 5, 4 mm ($\frac{3}{16}$in) crystal AB beads
- 1 sheet tracing paper
- machine sewing thread to match green fabric
- light box

### EMBROIDERY

*Careful counting will assist with the correct positioning of the embroidery and its motifs.*

1 Fold the fabric in half both ways. Run a line of tacking along the short fold. From the centre, work counted tacking over groups of three threads, along the long fold, out to the edges.

2 Count four threads down from the long tacked line. Remove the fifth thread across the fabric. Leave two threads, then remove another single thread.

3 From the centre, count 28 groups of three threads (84 threads) along the counted tacking. Using the Medium thread, work the first two lines of the merezhka pattern, along the length of the fabric, repeating the pattern as necessary.

*The scissors case shape will be cut from the completed embroidery, which continues into the seam allowance area.*

4 Remove threads as necessary, and work the remainder of the merezhka pattern.

5 Using three strands of the stranded cotton, work the zig-zagging line and the satin stitch motifs.

### CONSTRUCTION

1 Create two tracing paper pattern templates from the pattern on page 37. Make one full size, using the solid outline, and a smaller one using the inner dashed line. Mark the centre guide and dots on both templates.

2 Cut three full size pattern template pieces from the silk.

3 With the smaller template, cut one piece from the silk, and four from both the buckram and fusible webbing.

4 Following the manufacturer's instructions, iron the webbing onto the small piece of silk, and onto the centres of each of the three large pieces of silk.

5 Using the manufacturer's instructions, remove the webbing's paper, and iron a piece of buckram over each.

6 Fold the silk seam allowances over the buckram edges, and baste, easing the fullness in at the corners.

7 On a light box, using a dressmaker's pencil trace the full size pattern onto the embroidered panel, matching the centre line to the tacked guide, and centring it from top to bottom.

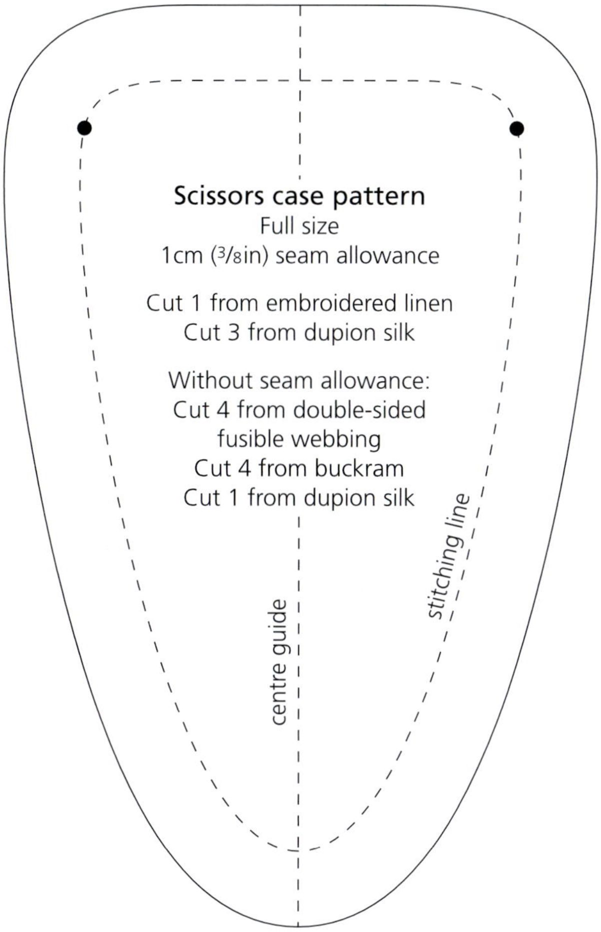


8 Using a sewing machine, zig-zag just inside the traced pattern shape, to stop fraying during construction.
9 Trim the fabric to the edge of the pattern shape.
10 Place the small silk/buckram piece behind the embroidered panel, with the silk facing it.
11 Fold the seam allowance over the buckram's edges, and baste in place, easing the fullness in at the corners.
12 Match two of the silk pieces, with wrong sides together, and neatly ladder stitch around the edge.
13 Match the embroidered panel to the remaining silk piece, with buckram sides together, and neatly ladder stitch around the edge.
14 Remove all basting.
15 Match the back of the embroidered panel to the silk panel. Starting at one dot, whip stitch the two pieces together, around the bottom. Finish at the other dot.

## MAKING THE CORD

1 Cut four 1.2 m (47 in) lengths from each of the pearl cottons. Matching their ends, knot them together.
2 Attach the knotted end to something stationary, such as a doorhandle, or a nail in a piece of wood.
3 At the loose end, separate the mauve threads from the green threads. Bundle the mauve threads and twist them until they want to twist back on themselves.

*Twist the threads in the same direction as they are already twisted, so that you are adding twist, not untwisting.*

4 Fasten the thread so that it cannot unwind.

*To fasten it, tape it to a table, or hold it in your teeth.*

5 Twist the green threads as much as the mauve ones.
6 Bring the two bundles together and knot them.
7 Carefully allow the threads to evenly twist together, to create a striped cord. Knot the end.
8 Next to each knot, bind the cord with machine sewing thread and take a few stitches through it to secure the ends. Cut off the knots.

## FINISHING

1 Starting at the top left of the case, insert the end of the cord into the top of the case, and fasten with small, strong, neat stitches.

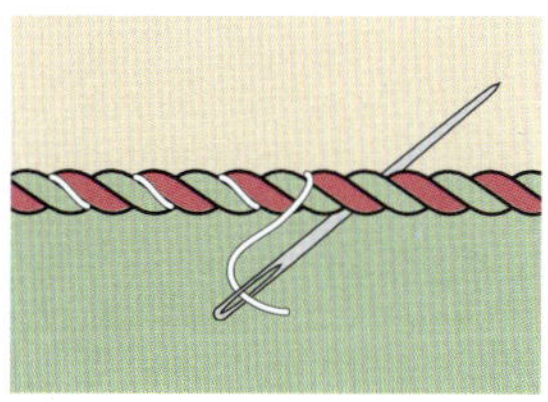

*Attach the cord by stitching around it and through the scissor case edge, so that the thread disappears between the twists in the cord, as shown in the diagram.*

2 Stitch the cord down around the bottom of the case, and up the other side. Then work across the top of the front of the case, and around the top of the back. Fasten the cord securely at the top of the right side of the case with a few strong stitches.
3 To make the hanging loop, insert the end of the cord in at the top left of the case, where the beginning end is. Neatly attach and bind the cord end with a few small, strong stitches.
4 Fasten some doubled machine sewing thread on the front of the bottom of the case. Thread the five crystal beads onto the thread. Take the thread through the top of the crystal teardrop and back through the five beads. Fasten the thread securely.

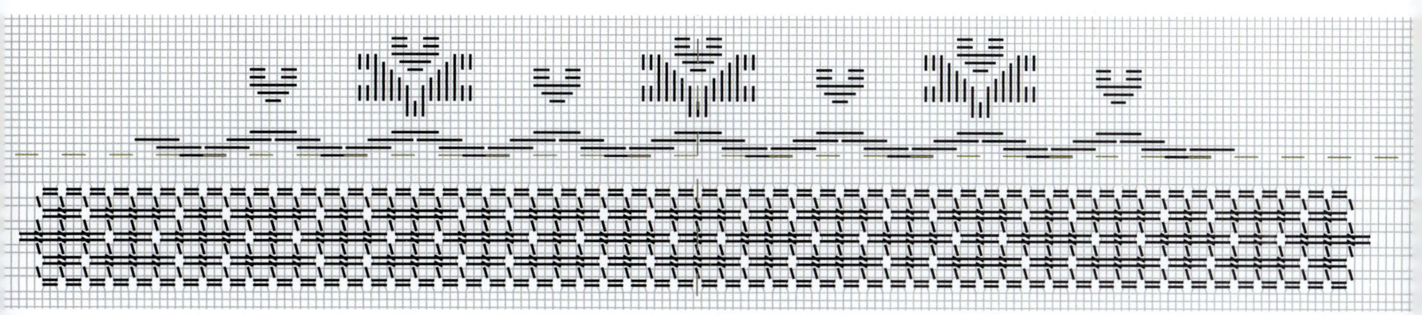

# Miniature pillow

**This sweet miniature pillow could be used as a brooch rest as shown, a pin cushion, or filled with dried flowers and herbs for a scented pillow.**

SIZE 11 x 11 cm (4 1/2 x 4 1/2 in)
TECHNIQUE Large scale Merezhka Poltavska
MATERIALS

- 20 x 20 cm (8 x 8 in) Glenshee linen, 29 count, stone/muffin*
- 23 m (25 yd) Medium thread, white (see 'Compatibility', p7)
- 1 skein each No 5 pearl cotton: DMC 778 (very light antique mauve), DMC 842 (very light beige brown)
- 2 squares blush pink satin fabric, 13.2 x 13.2 cm (5 3/16 x 5 3/16 in)
- small quantity of polyester fibre fill
- No 24 tapestry needle
- machine sewing thread to match linen

* *There are two products known as Glenshee linen, made by different manufacturers. The model is stitched using 'stone' from the UK. The closest US colour is 'muffin'.*

EMBROIDERY

❶ *Careful counting will assist with the correct positioning of the embroidery and its motifs.*

1 Fold the fabric in half both ways. From the centre, work counted tacking out to each edge, going under and over groups of four threads.
2 Work a square of counted tacking, centred over the guides, starting seven groups of four threads (28 threads) from the centre.

❶ *Each side has 14 groups of four threads (56 threads).*

3 Count out another five groups (20 threads) and work another square, with 24 groups of four threads (96 threads) along each side.

❶ *These two squares form the boundaries for the drawn thread area.*

4 At one of the centre guides, cut the outermost thread stretching across the drawn thread area. Withdraw each end of the thread back to the edges of the drawn thread area, and fasten them out of the way, with pins.

❶ *These thread ends will be sewn into the corners later, so do not cut them off.*

5 Work prutyk hemstitch, grouping together four threads, along the edge of this side of the square. When you reach the far end, unfasten the pinned thread.
6 Snip the outermost thread of the adjacent side at the centre guide. Withdraw it to the edges of the square, and fasten it out of the way.
7 Continuing with the same embroidery thread, hemstitch this next side, catching in the loose thread from the previous side, as part of the corner group of four.
8 Repeat until the outer edge of the square is complete.
9 At the inner edge of the drawn area, on each centre guide on each side, cut the first thread inside the area. Withdraw these threads ends to the edge of the drawn thread area, and fasten them out of the way.
10 Work prutyk hemstitch along each side of the inner edge of the drawn work area.
11 To work the layerings, more threads need to be withdrawn. At the centre guide, on the upper side of the square, leave two threads, cut two, leave two, cut two, leave two, cut two, leave two, cut two, and leave two (four cuts). Draw back the threads to the edges, and fasten them out of the way.
12 Starting seven chysnytsia right of the upper side, work the layerings for that entire side. Leave the threads hanging loose, ready to work the corner.
13 Work a wrapped bullion corner, according to the instructions on page 27.
14 Repeat for the remaining sides and corners, to complete the merezhka.

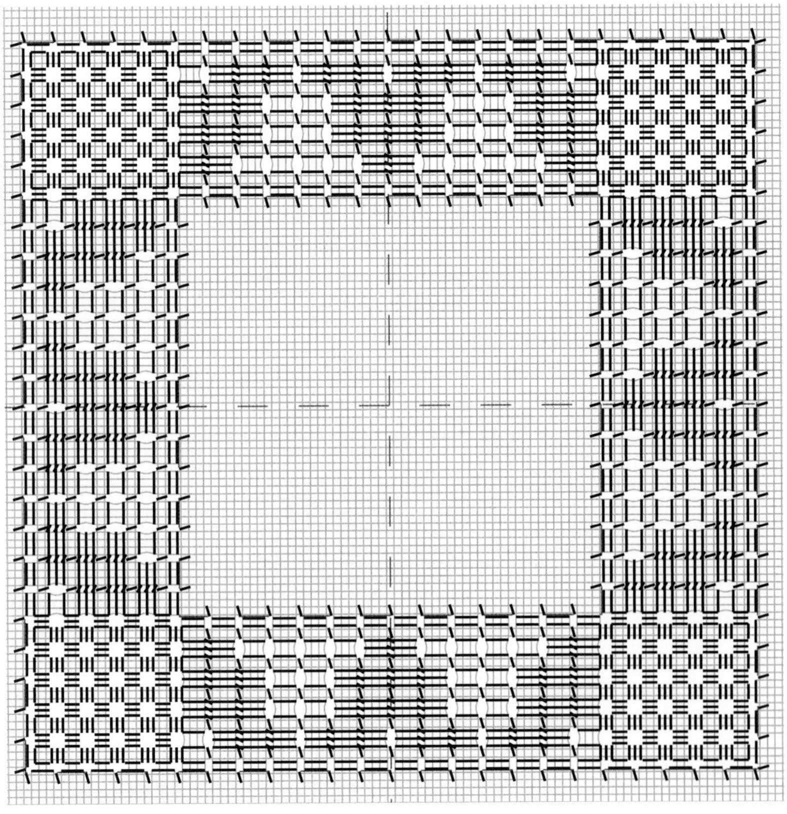

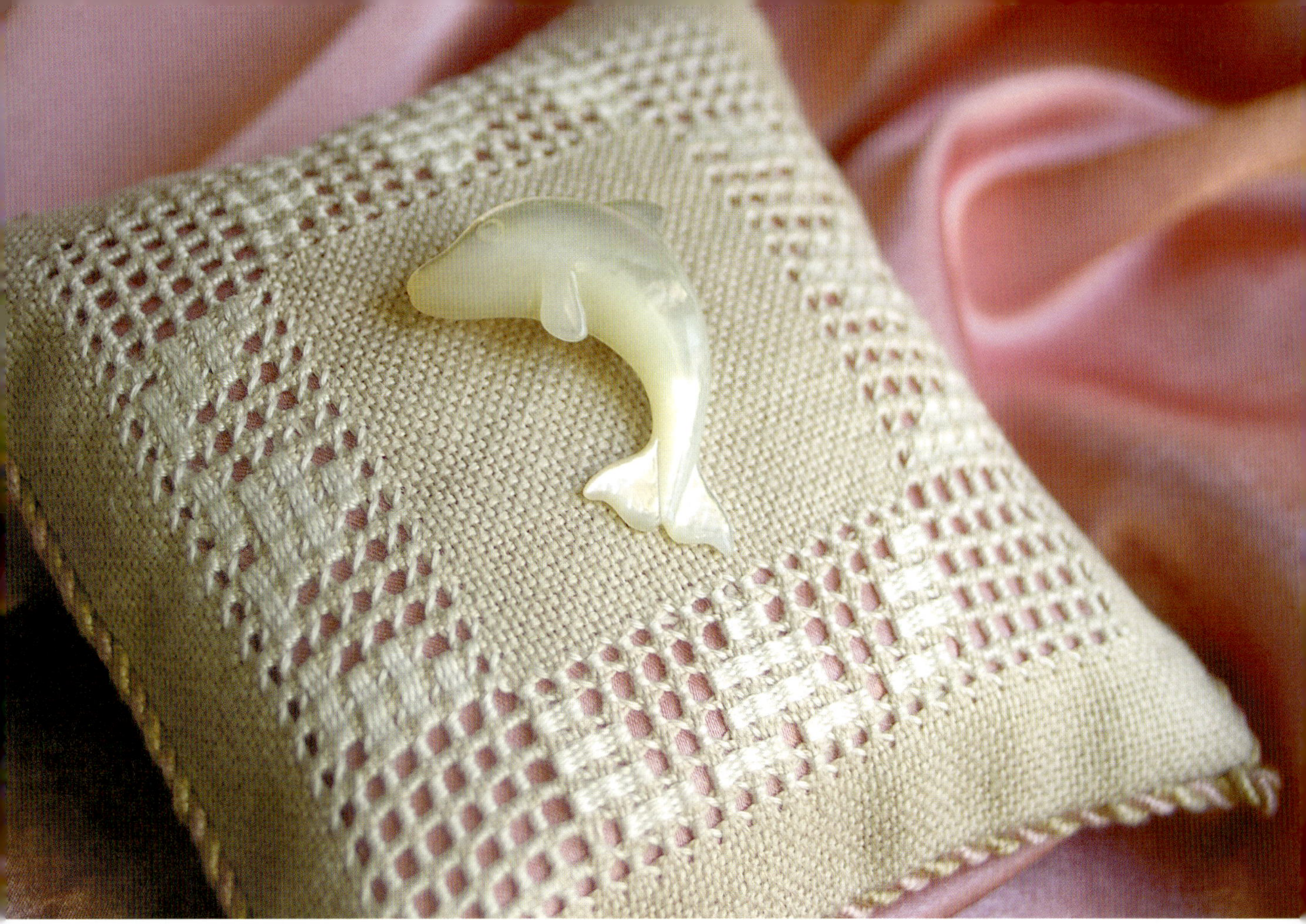

## MAKING THE CORD

1 Cut four 1 m (40 in) lengths from each of the pearl cottons. Matching their ends, knot them together.
2 Attach the knotted end to something stationary, such as a doorhandle, or a nail in a piece of wood.
3 At the loose end, separate the mauve threads from the brown threads. Bundle the mauve threads and twist them until they want to twist back on themselves.

❶ *Twist the threads in the same direction as they are already twisted, so that you are adding twist, not untwisting.*

4 Fasten the thread so that it cannot unwind.

❶ *To fasten it, tape it to a table, or hold it in your teeth.*

5 Twist the brown threads as much as the mauve ones.
6 Carefully allow the threads to evenly twist together, to create a striped cord. Knot the end.
7 Next to each knot, bind the cord with machine sewing thread, taking a few stitches through the cord, and wrapping it several times. Cut off the knots.

## CONSTRUCTION

1 Count 30 threads out from each edge of the embroidery, and trim, so that the fabric measures approximately 13.2 x 13.2 cm (5 3/16 x 5 3/16 in).
2 Baste one of the satin fabric squares to the back of the embroidery, so that the right side of the satin shows through the holes of the merezhka.
3 With the right sides together, sew the second piece of satin fabric to the embroidered panel, using a seam allowance of 1.2 cm (1/2 in). Leave a gap of 5 cm (2 in) in the centre of one of the sides, for turning.
4 Clip the corners, and turn the pillow the right way out. Stuff it with polyester fibre fill.

❶ *To make a scented pillow, fill it with dried flowers and herbs.*

5 Ladder stitch the gap closed, leaving a space of 5 mm (3/16 in) in the centre of the side.
6 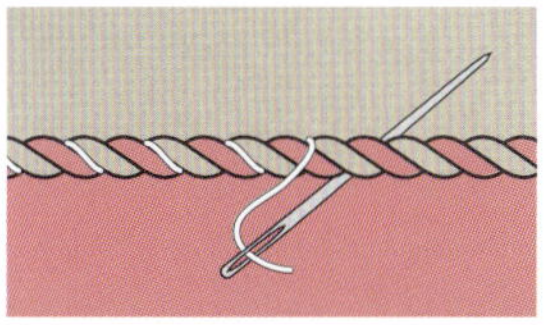
Tuck the cord end into the space. Attach the cord by stitching around the cord and through the pillow edge, so that the thread disappears between the twists in the cord, as shown in the diagram.
7 At each corner, knot the cord and fasten it with a few neat stitches.
8 Continue stitching the cord on, until it meets the small gap in the side of the pillow.
9 Trim the remaining cord to 1 cm (3/8 in). Insert the trimmed end of the cord into the small gap so that it slightly overlaps with the other end of the cord. Neatly stitch the gap closed. Finish stitching the cord to the pillow edge.

# Evening bag

**With funky ruffles, gold satin stitching and a geometric merezhka pattern, this little bag will team with any special outfit.**

**SIZE** 16 x 30 cm (6³/8 x 11⁷/8 in)
**TECHNIQUE** Small scale Merezhka Poltavska
**MATERIALS**

- 40 x 21 cm (16 x 8¹/4 in) 32ct linen, white
- 2 strips, 25 x 4 cm (10 x 1⁵/8 in) 32 count linen, white
- 46 m (50 yd) Thin thread, white (see 'Compatibility', p 7)
- 1 packet Madeira Decora #1455 or 1 skein DMC stranded cotton #738
- No 24 tapestry needle
- 21 x 34 cm (8¹/4 x 13³/8 in) gold satin fabric
- 5 x 55 cm (2 x 22 in) gold satin fabric
- machine sewing thread, white

**PREPARATION**

❶ *Careful counting will assist with the correct positioning of the embroidery and its motifs.*

1 Fold the long side of the fabric in half.
2 Along the fold, measure 5 cm (2 in) from one side of the fabric. Mark with a pin.
3 From the pin, work counted tacking over and under groups of three threads along the long side of the fabric, to the edges.
4 From the pin, count 25 threads down the fold. Mark with another pin.
5 From the new pin, work another line of counted tacking parallel to the previous one.
6 From the centre fold, count 61 groups of three threads (183 threads) towards each edge. Run a line of tacking across the short width of the fabric at this point, at each end.

❶ *The tacked guide lines form the boundaries for the merezhka band.*

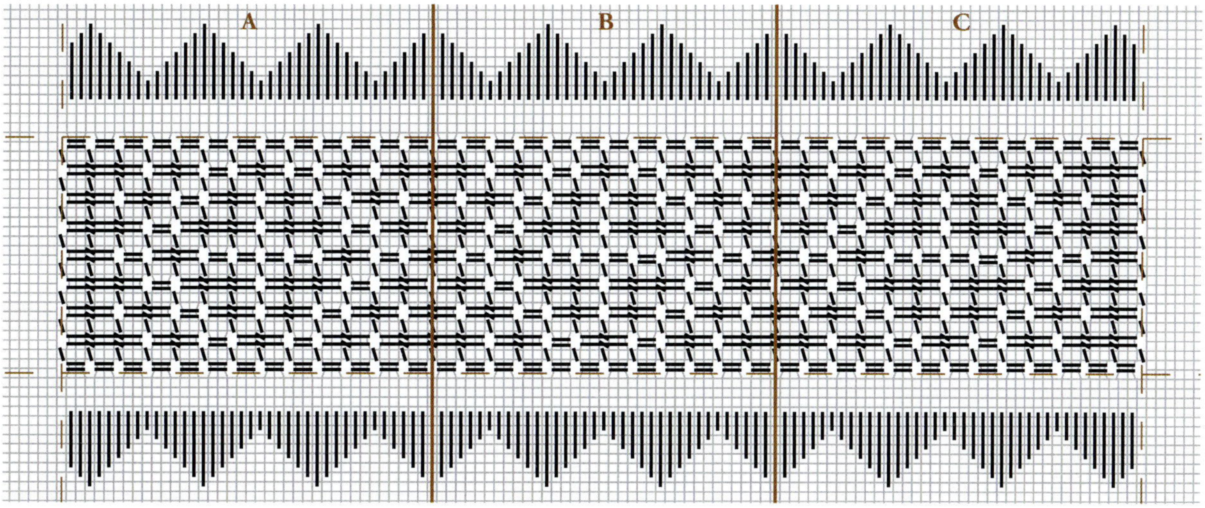


## EMBROIDERY

**The chart has three sections. A is the left end. B is the middle section, which is repeated eight times across the fabric. C is the right end.**

1 Along the length of the fabric, remove the first thread inside the counted tacking area. Leave two, then remove another. Stitch the entire first two lines.

2 Complete the remainder of the merezhka band.

3 Using 2 strands of the Decora or stranded floss, work the satin stitch sawtooth patterns along the top and bottom of the merezhka band, positioning the stitches according to the chart.

4 Remove all basting.

## CONSTRUCTION

❶ *Seam allowance is 1 cm (3/8 in), except where otherwise stated.*

1 With right sides facing, match the ends of the merezhka band together. Count in 3 threads from the ends of the bands, and machine sew down the bag side.

2 Trim the seam allowance to 1 cm (3/8 in). Zig-zag or overlock the seam allowance to neaten.

3 Machine sew across the base of the bag. Clip the corners.

4 With right sides together, fold the long side of the large piece of satin in half to create the bag lining. Machine sew down the side and across the bottom. Clip the corners.

5 Fold the linen strips in half along their length. Open out the fold, and fold each of the long edges in to meet the centre fold. Press.

6 Refold the original fold, so that the raw edges are inside the strip.

7 Machine sew down each side of the strips, 2 mm (1/8 in) from the edge, to create the handles.

8 To create the ruffle, match the short ends of the gold satin strip, with right sides together. Stitch. Fold the seam allowance open.

9 Fold the satin loop in half lengthwise, with the right side out.

10 Run two gathering lines around the entire loop, one 5 mm (3/16 in) and one 15 mm (5/8 in) away from the matched raw edges.

11 Gently and evenly pull the gathering threads to gather up the ruffle so that it fits snugly around the top of the bag.

12 With the bag right side out, align the seams and match the raw edges of the ruffle to the top of the bag, with the ruffle on the outside. Baste in place. Stitch.

13 Along the top edge, measure 4 cm (1 5/8 in) in from the sides of the bag, on the front and the back of the bag. Mark these four points with a pin.

14 On each side, place the handle ends over the pins, matching the raw edges with the top of the bag. Baste in place.

15 Slip the bag lining over the bag so that the right sides are facing. Match side seams.

16 Leaving a gap of 6 cm (2 3/8 in) on one side, stitch around the bag top.

17 Turn the bag lining through the gap and push it down inside the bag. Flip the handles and ruffle up.

18 Overstitch around the top of the bag, 2 mm (1/8 in) away from the ruffle.

# Climbing rose table runner

**This elegant table runner features two vines of climbing roses. The tapered ends of the runner are finished with tassels, for a contemporary touch.**

**SIZE** 23 x 85 cm (9 x 33½ in)
**TECHNIQUE** Small scale Merezhka Poltavska
**MATERIALS**

- 25 x 70 cm (10 x 27½ in) 32 count linen, white
- 90 m (100 yd) Thin thread, white (see 'Compatibility', p7)
- 25 x 70 cm (10 x 27½ in) unbleached linen fabric
- No 24 tapestry needle
- 2 tassels, 8.5 cm (3½ in) length, white
- machine sewing thread, white

## PREPARATION

❶ *Careful counting will assist with the correct positioning of the embroidery and its motifs.*

1 Fold the fabric in half both ways. Where the folds intersect is the centre. Mark with a pin.
2 On the short side, work counted tacking over and under groups of three threads, from the centre out to the fabric edges.

❶ *For this project, all counted tacking is worked with groups of three threads.*

3 Along the line of tacking, count out 16 groups of three threads (48 threads) from the centre, to each side. Mark each side with a pin.
4 From the pins, along the fabric length, work counted tacking to the edges.
5 On the original tacked line, count a further 12 groups plus 1 thread (37 threads) from the pins, to each side. Mark these points with pins.
6 From the new pins, along the fabric length, work counted tacking out to the edges.

❶ *There are two parallel lines stretching down each side of the fabric length.*

7 From the original line of tacking, count 30 groups of three threads (90 threads) each way down the runner length, and run lines of counted tacking across the width.
8 Count a further 30 groups (90 threads) each way down the length of the runner and run lines of counted tacking across the width.
9 At one end of the fabric, counting from the guides just inserted, count 16 groups of three (48 threads), and run a line of counted tacking across.

❶ *This tacked guide forms the bottom end of the design.*

10 At the other end, count out 15 groups of three (45 threads), and run a line of counted tacking across.

❶ *This tacked guide forms the top end of the design.*

## EMBROIDERY

**The chart has three sections. A is the top section. B, the middle section, is repeated four times down the length of the fabric. C is the bottom section. Each part fits within the counted tacking sections.**

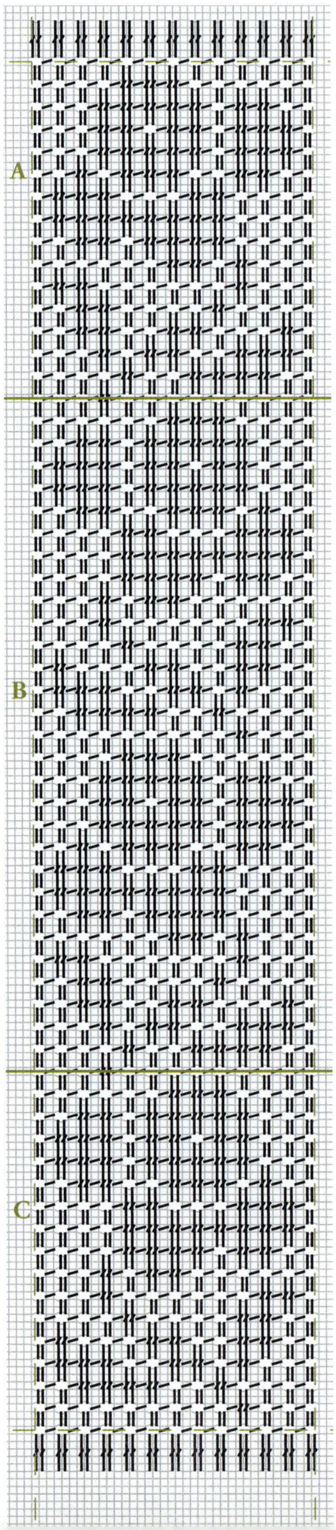


1 Work lines of Roman stitches just above section A and below section C.
2 Remove the first thread down the entire length of one of the drawn thread areas, leave two, then remove another. Work the entire first two lines, paying careful attention to the positioning of the motifs. Check that the correct stitches line up with the end of each tacked section.
3 Complete the rest of the design.
4 Repeat the design down the other side of the fabric.

## CONSTRUCTION

1 Fold the ends of the runner in half to find their centres. Mark with pins.
2 Measure 12.5 cm (5 in) from the end, down each side of the runner. Mark each point with a pin.
3 Diagonally draw a line between the pin at the end of the runner, and the pins 12.5 cm (5 in) from the end.
4

Cut along the lines.

5 Repeat for the unbleached linen backing fabric.
6 With right sides together, match the edges of the two pieces.
7 Leaving a gap of 10 cm (4 in) in one of the long sides, sew around the runner, using a seam allowance of 1 cm (3/8 in). Clip the corners and turn right side out through the gap.
8 Neatly ladder stitch the gap closed.
9 Sew one tassel to each end of the runner, at the pointed tips.

# Swirls doily

**This doily features a very contemporary design. The project makes no claims of being traditional in style, rather it is a modern interpretation of the technique.**

SIZE 33 x 37 cm (13 x 14 3/4 in)
TECHNIQUE Large scale Merezhka Poltavska
MATERIALS

- 43 x 47 cm (17 x 18 1/2 in) 25 count Legacy linen, brilliant white
- 138 m (150 yd) Thick thread, white (see 'Compatibility', p7)
- No 22 tapestry needle
- Dressmaker's pencil, blue
- machine sewing thread. white

## PREPARATION

❶ *Careful counting will assist with the correct positioning of the embroidery and its motifs.*

1 Fold the fabric in half both ways. Where the folds intersect is the centre. Mark with a pin.
2 Work counted tacking with groups of four threads, from the centre out to the fabric edges. Remove the pin.

❶ *For this project, all counted tacking is worked with groups of four threads.*

3 On the short side, count 14 groups of four, plus three threads (59 threads) from the centre towards each edge. Mark these points with a pin.
4 Count out a further 40 threads along the guide, to each side and mark with a pin.
5 Count another 52 threads along the guide, out to each side, and mark with a pin.
6 Count out a further 48 threads along the guide, to each side and mark with a pin.
7 Run lines of counted tacking perpendicular to the centre guide, from the each of the pins out to the edge.
8 On the long side, count 20 groups of four, plus one thread (81 threads) from the centre towards each edge. Mark these points with a pin.
9 Count out a further 40 threads along the guide, to each side and mark with a pin.
10 Count another 52 threads along the guide, out to each side, and mark with a pin.
11 Count out a further 48 threads along the guide, to each side and mark with a pin.
12 Run lines of counted tacking perpendicular to the centre guide, from the each of the pins out to the edge.

❶ *Check the position of counted tacking guides against the diagram, right. If any are wrong, correct them.*

## EMBROIDERY

❶ *Refer to the diagram right, and to the mitred layerings corner instructions on page 26.*

1 The drawn thread area is bounded by the guide lines A and B. Between these two guides, cut and draw back the first thread on the inside and outside edges of this area. Fasten the threads out of the way.

❶ *Refer to the chart on page 46.*

2 Work prutyk hemstitching along the inside and outside edges of the drawn thread area

❶ *Each chysnytsia has four threads, except for the corner ones, which have five threads, at both the inside and outside edges.*

3 Start at the solid pink line on the chart, and work the merezhka design, cutting and drawing back the threads shown in the diagram below, as necessary.
4 Upon reaching a corner, work the mitred layerings corners as described on page 26.
5 Continue around the band, until the stitching meets up with the beginning.

## HEMS

1 On the side of guide line C that is closest to the centre, cut the first thread at the centre guides, and draw back the ends to where the C guide lines intersect.
2 Trim the fabric along guide line D, and remove any of the remaining tacking thread from guide line D.
3 The fabric between the removed thread and the edge is the hem allowance.
4 Work the mitred hem corners according to the instructions on page 30.
5 Tack the hems in place.
6 Hemstitch the hems, using the prutyk method described on page 28.

❶ *Ensure that all the threads align properly with themselves through the fold, so that there is no puckering, and the hem sits flat.*

7 Remove all the tacking.

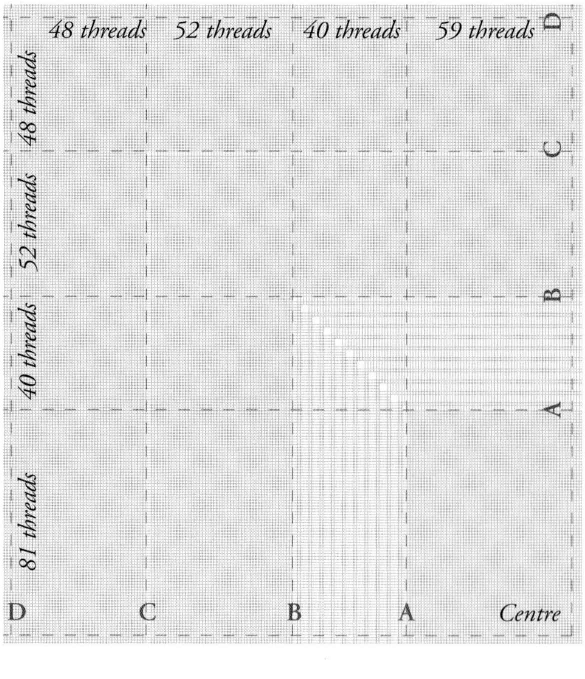

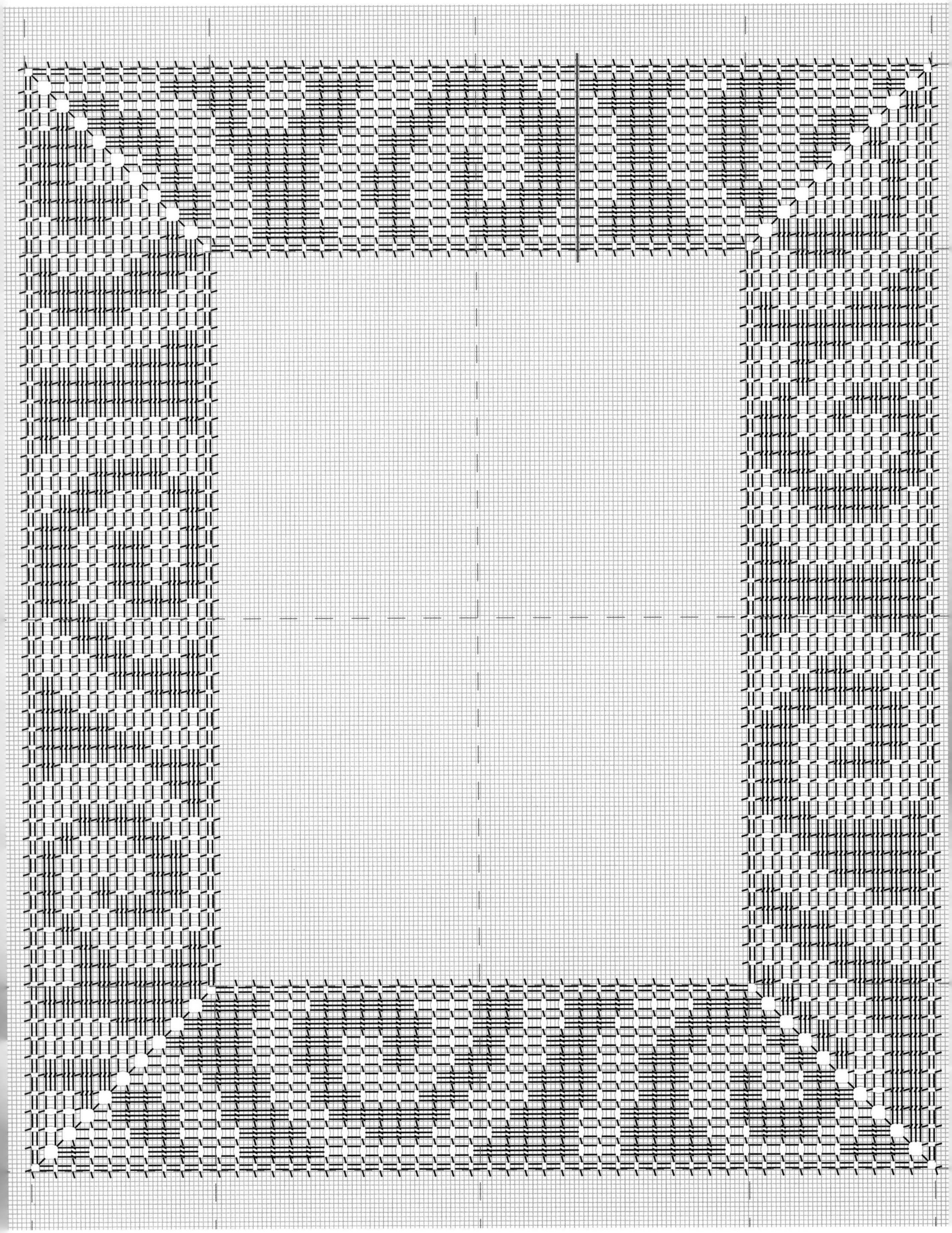

# Merezhka supplies

Most of the products listed in this book are readily available in your favourite local and on-line needlework shops.

If you are having any difficulty finding any of the products, you may like to contact that product's closest distributor (listed below) to locate a local shop from which to order.

## Thread

### ANCHOR

**Semco Crafts, Australia**
Tel: +61 2 8543 4300
www.semco.com.au

**Coats Crafts, UK**
Tel: +44 1325 394237
www.coatscrafts.co.uk

**Coats GmbH, Germany**
Tel: +49 7644 802 287
www.coatsgmbh.de

### DMC

**Radda, Australia**
Tel: +61 2 9559 3088
www.radda.com.au

**DMC Creative World Ltd, UK**
www.dmc.com

**DMC Incorporated, USA**
*Distributors of DMC thread, except coton à broder.*
Tel: +1 973 589 0606
www.dmc-usa.com

**Lacis, USA**
*Suppliers of DMC coton à broder.*
Tel: +1 510 843 7178
www.lacis.com

**DMC, France**
Tél: 03 89 31 91 89
www.dmc.com

### MADEIRA

**SSS Pty Ltd, Australia**
Tel: 1300 888 778
www.sewingcraft.com

**Madeira UK Ltd, UK**
Tel: +44 1765 640 003
www.madeira.co.uk

**Madeira USA**
Tel: +1 603 528 2944
www.madeirausa.com

**Madeira Garnfabrik KG, Germany**
Tel: +49 761 5 10 40 0
www.madeira.de

### PRESENCIA

**Presencia Australia**
Tel: +61 2 6241 8382
www.presencia.com.au

**Presencia UK**
Tel: +44 1634 711228
www.bigginslace.co.uk

**Presencia USA**
Tel (toll-free): 866 277 6364
www.presenciausa.com

**Presencia Hilaturas SA, Spain**
Tel: +34 96 245 51 25
www.presencia-hilaturas.es

### WEEKS DYE WORKS

**Weeks Dye Works, Inc. USA**
Tel (toll-free): 877.OVERDYE
www.weeksdyeworks.com

## Linen

### GLENSHEE

**Elizabeth Prickett, UK**
www.ruskinlace.org.uk/glenshee.htm

**The Heart's Content, Inc. USA**
Tel: +1 920 494 9434
www.theheartscontent.com

### LEGACY

**Access Commodities Inc. USA**
Tel: +1 972 563 3313
Fax: +1 972 563 3330

### PERMIN

**Ireland Needlecraft, Australia**
Tel: +61 3 9702 3222
www.irelandneedlecraft.com.au

**Michael Whitaker Fabrics Ltd UK**
Tel: +44 1535 636903

**Wichelt Imports, Inc. USA**
Toll Free: 800 356 9516
www.wichelt.com

**Carl J. Permin A/S, Denmark**
Tel: +45 3672 1200
www.permin.dk

### ZWEIGART

**Radda, Australia**
Tel: +61 2 9559 3088
www.radda.com.au

**Zweigart UK**
Tel: +44 1889 585666
www.heritagestitchcraft.co.uk

**Zweigart, USA**
Tel: +1 732 562 8888
www.zweigart.com

**Zweigart & Sawitzki, Germany**
Tel: +49 7031 795 5
www.zweigart.de

Merezhka supplies are also available from:

**Vetty Creations**
PO Box 1723
Hornsby Westfield NSW 1635
Australia
Tel/Fax: +61 2 9477 5214
yvette@vettycreations.com.au
www.vettycreations.com.au

## Further reading


Eaton, Gay. *Ukrainian Whitework*, Gay Eaton, Dunedin, New Zealand, 2005.

Kmit, Ann; Luciow, Johanna; Luciow, Loretta. *Ukrainian Embroidery*, Ukrainian Gift Shop Inc., N.E. Minneapolis, MA USA, 1984.

Kulynych-Stakhurska, Olena. *The Art of Ukrainian Embroidery: Techniques and Technology*, Misioner, Lviv, Ukraine, 1996.

Kutsenko, Maria. *Ukrainian Embroideries*, Spectrum Publications, Richmond, VIC, Australia, 1977.

O'Neill, Tania D. *Ukrainian Embroidery Techniques*, STO Publications, Mountaintop, PA USA, 1984.

Ruryk, Nancy. *Ukrainian Embroidery Stitches and Designs*, The Ukrainian Women's Association of Canada, 1978 (4th ed).

Wolynetz, Lubow. *The Tree of Life, The Sun, The Goddess: Symbolic Motifs in Ukrainian Folk Art*, The Ukrainian Museum, New York, NY USA, 2005.

# Index

Page numbers in **bold** refer to pages which also include photographs or illustrations.



# Glossary

**chysnytsia** – threads that are bundled together, usually in groups of three or four. Plural: chysnytsi

**double prutyk** – hemstitching down both sides of the space where a thread has been removed.

**merezhka** – general Slavic language term for 'drawn thread work'. Plural: merezhky

**oblast** – province.

**Poltava** – city in Eastern Ukraine.

**prutyk** – hemstitching along the edge of the space where a thread has been removed.

**rushnyk** – (pronounced 'rooshnik') embroidered ritual cloth with spiritual significance used for everyday life, holidays and ceremonies. Plural: rushnyky.